Musical Ability in Children and its Measurement

Musical Ability in Children
and its Measurement

ARNOLD BENTLEY
B.A., Ph.D., A.R.C.M., L.R.A.M.

Senior Lecturer in Music in Education
Department of Education
University of Reading

GEORGE G. HARRAP & CO. LTD
London · Toronto · Wellington · Sydney

First published in Great Britain 1966
by GEORGE G. HARRAP & CO. LTD
182 High Holborn, London, W.C.1

Reprinted 1966

Composed in Ehrhardt type and printed by
W. & J. Mackay & Co. Ltd, Chatham
Made in Great Britain

Preface

This book is about the musical abilities of young children and attempts to measure them. There is no lack of opinion about the abilities of the young, but it is usually based upon subjective assessments of individual pupils by their teachers. Such opinion is valuable; however, it is inevitably restricted to a teacher's experience with a comparatively limited number of pupils. Factual information, as distinct from opinion, was the aim of the research about to be described, information that might be of use to those engaged in music education.

In the course of the research the musical abilities of large numbers of children were examined by objective methods; a new battery of group-tests was devised with young children primarily in mind. These tests measure certain types of judgments that are proposed as fundamental to musical activities; they are not concerned with the aesthetic aspects of musical enjoyment, nor with the question of whether the child 'likes' music or not; nor do they measure any of the motor skills specifically required for the various forms of instrumental playing.

In writing this book I have avoided, wherever possible, technical terms with which many teachers and musicians might not be familiar. Furthermore, the book is short. This is intentional, in the hope that the potentially interested reader, and particularly the busy teacher, will not be discouraged from embarking upon reading it by sheer bulk. Its subject is fundamental, thought-challenging, and of importance to anyone who teaches children and music. It contains facts, ideas, controversial assumptions, and speculation. It may provide an introduction to an important and fascinating field of study, and I hope that the reader will be provoked to consult at least some of the references quoted.

I should like to acknowledge the debt that my own work owes to that of previous investigators, especially to the tests and extensive writings of Dr H. D. Wing, with whom I have additionally had the advantage of personal discussion and correspondence. I am also indebted to Dr R. N. Curnow, Dr R. P. G. Shuter, and my wife for reading the typescript of this book and making helpful suggestions. For his indefatigable work in connection with the making of the final recordings of the tests described in Chapter VI[1] Mr John Fry, of George G. Harrap & Co., Ltd, has earned my warmest thanks. Finally, for their co-operation throughout the investigations, I thank numerous teachers in schools, and even more numerous children, including my own.

A.B.

Reading, 1965

---

[1] *Measures of Musical Abilities* (Arnold Bentley—George G. Harrap). A disc recording of the four tests of the battery.

Contents

analysis—Other abilities considered—No attempt to measure musical ability *in toto*; Summary of basic assumptions underlying the tests selected

Need for specially devised tests—Description of the pilot tests—Some information about the children who worked the tests—Results of the testing— Discussion of the results

Pitch discrimination test—Memory tests, tonal and rhythmic—Chord analysis test—Recording and reproduction—Instructions and examples—The answer form—Order of presentation of the tests— Administration of the battery—Texts of the instructions for the tests

Validity—Reliability—Relationships between the individual tests of the battery—Influence of sex— Influence of intelligence

Test battery scores in relation to chronological age— Disclosure of wide range of musical abilities at any given age—Musical Ability Age—Musical abilities

appear to be largely innate—Grading of scores—
Interpretation of the grades

Relative difficulty of the tests—Pitch discrimination
—Memory: Tonal memory—Rhythmic memory—
Chord analysis—Summary of findings

Interpretation and speculation—The purpose of
music-teaching in school—Sex and musical abilities
—Intelligence, chronological age, and musical
abilities—Chord analysis—Memory—Pitch discrimination—Postscript

Tables

1 *Musical Ability and its Measurement*

What is musical ability?—Lack of a definition—Is it analysable or an indivisible unity?—Is it inherited or acquired?—Need for specificity in measurement—A compromise—Limits set to the present work

WHAT IS MUSICAL ABILITY?

What is musical ability? There is no simple answer. We might suggest the following: that characteristic, or those characteristics, which distinguish 'musical' persons from 'unmusical' persons. But how shall we define 'musical' as distinct from 'unmusical'? We well know that some persons are more 'musical' than others; but how and where do we draw the dividing line?

Furthermore, in what ways do those whom we know as 'musical' exhibit their 'musicalness'? They may be composers, performers, or listeners, or all three. The person who composes music may be safely regarded as musical, even if there are differences of opinion about the quality of his compositions. The performer who never composes

M.A.C.—B

may also be safely regarded as musical, although in a different way; he re-creates in sound the ideas the composer has imaged and recorded in the score by means of visual symbols. The listener who neither composes nor performs may also be a musical person; for the composer's ideas, recreated in sound by the performer, still have no meaning until they have been heard and understood by the attentive listener.

All three, composer, performer, and attentive listener, are 'musical'; all three possess characteristics that distinguish them from those who neither compose, nor perform, nor listen to music. In so far as they are all actively participating in a musical experience they may be said to have musical ability. But what are their distinguishing characteristics?

LACK OF A DEFINITION

The difficulty is that there is no generally agreed criterion or definition of musical ability. Many attempts have been made to understand it and to measure it, but the nature of these attempts depends more upon belief than scientifically proved conclusions. Incontrovertible, scientifically proved conclusions concerning musical ability and its nature are elusive. The factual information gained from controlled experiments may be indisputable; but the experiments themselves are based upon certain assumptions. And synonyms for assumption are words such as postulation, proposition, speculation—words implying an element of opinion, point of view, belief. We are still in the 'credo' stage.

Let us consider briefly a few of the assumptions concerning the nature of musical ability, and how it is acquired.

IS IT ANALYSABLE OR AN INDIVISIBLE UNITY?

There are those[1] who maintain that music is a unity, and musical ability a single, albeit complex, ability. Others[2] would analyse music into component parts, and think in terms of groups of separate abilities such as pitch discrimination, sense of time, of rhythm, of timbre, of loudness, of harmony, and so on.

IS IT INHERITED OR ACQUIRED?

Then, again, some believe that musical ability, or abilities, are largely inherited; others that they are acquired after birth. Those who subscribe to the idea of inherited ability admit the importance of environment for the development of what has been inherited; those who discount inherited abilities still admit different degrees of "biological predisposition".[3]

These are extreme views. Arguments are propounded for both, but none is entirely convincing. Nature and nurture, inherited talent and development within the environment, are not entirely independent. The child who is born with superior musical talents, or "biological predisposition", into an environment that is wholly unfavourable is not likely to develop his innate capacity. On the other hand, however favourable the environment, the child with little innate capacity is unlikely to make much progress in musical activities. There is plenty of evidence for this last statement. It may be seen in any school age-group whose members are subject to very similar environmental background and identical class teaching; the different

[1] For instance, Mursell (1931) and Wing (1948).
[2] For instance, Seashore (1938).
[3] For instance, Lundin (1953).

rates of progress of individuals are most marked. Evidence of similar differences in the rate of progress of children of the same age and similar home environment may be obtained from studio teachers of instrumental playing. Perhaps even more notable are the differences observed in children of the same parents in a 'musical' home. One child may make rapid progress in musical activities, another only modest progress, another none at all. The environment, opportunities, encouragement, quality of tuition, are similar for all the children of the family; what each child individually makes of these seems to depend, in very large measure, upon some innate capacity, native talent, "biological predisposition", or whatever we choose to call it.

In discussing the musical abilities of young children, and in the attempts to measure them, we shall adopt the point of view that all children may have something to gain from some sort of participation in music, from listener-only to highly skilled instrumental or vocal performer, or even composer; that no child should be denied whatever pleasure, satisfaction, and self-fulfilment he can obtain from music; but that, whatever the cause, be it heredity, environment, or a combination of these, and, however much the egalitarian may dislike the idea, children both at an early age and subsequently show widely differing abilities, or degrees of ability, in music.

NEED FOR SPECIFICITY IN MEASUREMENT

Can these varying abilities, or degrees of ability, be measured? Measurement implies comparison; it involves numerical quantities. Can such be applied to music? Any attempts to apply specific, objective measurement to human beings and human behaviour tend to arouse controversy. Attempts to apply such measurements in the aesthetic sphere are particularly open to challenge, and this is even more especially so in music. Since music is essentially sound-moving-in-time it cannot be considered even in the same way, for instance, as the more static painting, piece of sculpture, or other work of art. The power of music being primarily emotive, such challenge must be accepted as inevitable. However, if the attempts to measure and the ensuing criticisms of such attempts together result in any useful addition to knowledge, even if it be firmly negative, then the attempts are justified.

Assuming, then, that measurement may be attempted, what exactly is to be measured? This question takes us back to our earlier statement that there is no generally agreed criterion or definition of musical ability, and to the conflicting points of view as to whether, on the one hand, music is a unity and musical ability a single, although complex, ability, or, on the other hand, music is analysable into several component parts, and the abilities corresponding to these parts are separately measurable.

Seashore, whose "Measures of Musical Talent" (1939) are perhaps the most widely known of all musical ability tests, worked from the point of view that music is analysable into its component parts, and that a "hierarchy of talents" corresponding to these parts could be measured. Furthermore, Seashore maintained that these talents are innate; his use of the word 'talents' was intentional. He was a pioneer in musical-ability testing. Inevitably his work has been challenged. Some of the criticisms are misguided as a result of inadequate reading of his writings; some of his critics have attributed wider claims for his "Measures" than he himself made, and then proceeded to try to disprove them. Seashore himself constantly pointed out the limitations of his "Measures" and the fact that they did not measure the whole of musical ability.

Subscribers to the point of view that music is a unity, and musical ability a single, if complex, ability, are the chief critics of Seashore and his analytical measurements. They maintain that analysis destroys music, and that tests of musical ability should consist of acknowledged musical material and not merely the elements of it, as, of course, is the case with Seashore's "Measures". But the use of acknowledged musical material in a group test introduces the affective and intellectual aspects; judgments become complicated, and it becomes much more difficult for the subjects to know exactly what they are supposed to do; with young children confusion results.

If measurement is to be made, both that which is measured and the terms in which it is to be measured must be specific. We can measure in inches, in ounces, in litres, separately and specifically; but there is no single, composite, meaningful measure of all three together. Similarly in music: pitch and time factors, loudness, timbre, concurrent sounds, are all part of the musical whole; they can all be measured separately, but for the whole musical experience a single specific term of measurement does not exist. As will be seen later, even the pitch and time factors—*i.e.*, only two of the many involved—may cause confusion when attempts are made to measure them in combination.

It is interesting to note that, in spite of their criticisms of the analytical approach, when the adherents of the 'music is a unity' school of thought themselves attempt to measure musical ability the very complexity of this ability compels them to use separate tests of the different factors of it.

It has to be accepted that the measurement of musical ability has not yet progressed beyond a rather rudimentary and unsatisfactory stage. Nor could it be otherwise whilst there exists no agreement on what musical ability is. We may be able to recognize it, or think we can, but we cannot as yet define it.

A COMPROMISE

What, then, can be done? It seems that we must compromise. It may not, as yet, be possible to prove either that musical ability is an inherited talent, or that it is entirely acquired during the separate lifetime of the individual. This need be no serious disadvantage, for we know well enough that in spite of comparable age, environment, and opportunity children vary enormously in progress in musical activities. Whether musical ability is a single whole or whether it is analysable is still very much a matter of speculation. But because no satisfactory means have been found of measuring the whole, this is no valid reason for not trying to discover what we can about some of the parts of the whole.

LIMITS SET TO THE PRESENT WORK

In our attempts to discover and measure the musical abilities of young children we must constantly keep in mind that these children are relatively inexperienced and, for the most part, untrained musically. The abilities with which we shall be concerned are such as the child may have inherited and/or acquired, in the main incidentally and not through specific musical training. Therefore such abilities as are measured must be basic and elemental.

Since it is through active participation in music that children most commonly acquire musical experience, we shall further restrict ourselves to the investigation of such abilities as are basic and essential to progress in active music-making as vocalist and instrumentalist—*i.e.*, to the performance of music.

We shall try to discover trends of abilities amongst young children in general; therefore as many children as possible must be studied. Since large numbers are involved the techniques of group-testing must be used. This imposes certain restrictions, but against these may be set the advantages of information obtained from large numbers such as it would be impossible to obtain by individual-testing techniques.

Within the limits of these restrictions we have to decide what musical abilities, or aspects of musical ability, we can and wish to measure. Having decided upon these, we must devise tests that will reveal not so much what we think children should be able to do, but what in fact they can do.

Therefore, in the first place, we must consider the musical development of children in their early years. Observation of the abilities that are developing spontaneously will give some indication as to what are the basic, elemental abilities in music, and will also suggest how and at what stage of development we may profitably start measuring these abilities.

It will also be necessary to consider the advantages, limitations, and conditions of the methods of measurement to be used—*i.e.*, group-tests.

2 Musical Development of Children in their Early Years[1]

The first appeal of music—Apprehension of melody—Stage of analysis—Essential elements of melody—Responses of children to the rhythm and tonal configuration of melody—Importance of memory

THE FIRST APPEAL OF MUSIC

Music's appeal to the young child is immediate and direct. His response to it is spontaneous from infancy onward. In early infancy the main attraction would seem to be the quality of the sounds: the pleasant sound of Mother singing, the tinkle of the bell, possibly the sound of instruments like the violin or the pianoforte.

At the same time, or soon afterwards, the rhythmic element of music causes the child to react by bodily response, varying in degree from indiscriminate bodily movement to a complete identification of movement with the pulse of the music.

[1] For accounts of early development in music see, for example, Revesz (1953, pp. 171–176), Farnsworth (1958, pp. 196–199), and Schoen (1940, pp. 220–234).

APPREHENSION OF MELODY

Later the element of melody is apprehended—*i.e.*, the succession of pitch sounds within a rhythmic framework. When a tune or figure that has been previously heard is subsequently recognized, memory for melody is established. The mind has grasped and retained a particular organization of tonal and rhythmic elements that is different, and recognizably so, from any other organization of these elements. What may previously have been a meaningless succession of sounds, however pleasing, has now become a meaningful, recognizable delineation.

With increasing experience more melodies are apprehended and remembered, with increasing clarity of detail. Rather vague, indeterminate upward and downward pitch movement, merely suggesting the tune, gradually becomes the specific upward- or downward-moving intervals of the tune. No longer is it an approximation; it *is* the tune.

Evidence of this is plentiful in the spontaneous singing of the infant and the very young child. As he sings to himself at play he extemporizes, but sometimes we hear recognizable fragments of tune. As the child grows these fragments increase in length, until 'whole' tunes are remembered and sung accurately in terms of both pitch and rhythm. The process seems to be one of continually increasing clarification.

In this, as in all else, different children proceed at different speeds. Some can remember, musically, far more effectively than others of the same age. But, whatever the chronological age, when a child can remember a musical tune accurately he has reached a specific stage of development. The buzzing confusion, formerly only dimly perceived, has become a specific, unique musical experience; the details, as integral parts of the whole, have become clear.

Much progress has been made; but, having reached this stage, some people appear to make no further progress. The memory span may be extended to embrace longer tunes as they are presented, especially if they are presented often enough. Commercial 'popular' entertainment relies almost entirely on this ability to remember a tune, and ensures that it is presented often enough within a short space of time to be remembered. Repetition, appropriately varied, is the essence of form in music whether 'serious' or 'popular'.

The mere extension of the memory span obviously assists the enjoyment of music, and for this kind of enjoyment, involving little more than elementary emotional reaction to the sounds that are heard, it is not necessary to proceed away from this stage.

STAGE OF ANALYSIS

However, the process of clarification that has already begun must continue if the child is to make music for himself. Given the opportunity and simple instruments he will do this. When he thinks he is unobserved he will often do it merely through singing. His vocal or instrumental improvisations become less and less rhapsodic and take on a simple form, if only one of apparently endless repetition. Moreover, he appears to become increasingly interested in detail. When the tune is wrong, and when he realizes this and attempts to put it right, he has become conscious of a point of important detail—*i.e.*, the pitch or time interval. He has reached a stage at which he can isolate

from the whole tune a rhythmic figure or an interval in pitch—
i.e., a stage of analysis.

By whatever kind of experience or tuition this point may be
reached, reached it must be if further progress in musical
education is to continue. Analysis of the Gestalt, whether it be
a whole tune, phrase, or figure, into its component intervals
must take place if the child is to achieve the means of exploring
music independently. The learning and recognition of the
musical intervals accepted by his particular social culture is an
essential stage in musical development.

ESSENTIAL ELEMENTS OF MELODY

In its basic form music is melody, earlier defined as a "succession of pitch sounds within a rhythmic framework." To
apprehend a melody the subject must be able to remember
sounds already heard in order to relate to them sounds currently being heard and those that are to follow. "Music . . .
is a subjective phenomenon depending on the activity of the
listener's mind . . . it only begins when the heard sounds are
recognized as possessing a meaningful relation to each other."[1]
Sounds have a "meaningful relation" to each other primarily in
terms of pitch intervals and note-lengths—*i.e.*, the tonal and
rhythmic elements. Timbre and degree of loudness may affect
the aesthetic aspect of performance, but they are not of such
fundamental importance as the tonal and rhythmic elements.
The same tune is recognizable whether played on the piccolo
or the tuba, loudly or softly. Its recognizability depends in-
herently not upon timbre, nor upon the degree of loudness,
nor even upon its absolute pitch, but upon its constituent

[1] Lowery, 1952, p. 18.

relative pitch and note-lengths. If these are the same the tune is the same; if these are not the same the tune is different. In the apperception of the tonal element of melody pitch discrimination is involved.

RESPONSES OF CHILDREN TO THE RHYTHM AND TONAL CONFIGURATION OF MELODY

Response to the rhythmic and tonal elements of melody may be observed in almost any group of children. In rhythmic activities when a pronounced rhythmic figure has asserted itself the majority of the group quickly seize upon that figure, without instruction, and join in the group participation in the figure as one person. The individuals as it were coalesce rhythmically into the dominant rhythmic pattern. This may be seen not only in the class-room but when children are playing together quite spontaneously.[1]

The tonal element of melody commonly elicits from children a vocal response—*i.e.*, they join in the singing of the tune they hear. However, unison singing, which is a vocal response using exactly the same tonal configuration as that of the stimulus tune, at the same pitch level, seems to occur less spontaneously, and at a later stage, than coalescence upon a rhythmic figure. How the unison may occur is illustrated in the following paragraph; this is no more than a single example of what may be observed in the larger groups of school class-rooms.

Two small sisters frequently sang as they played. Their singing, mainly improvisatory, was usually independent, at different pitches and using different tonal configurations.

[1] For examples see Moorhead and Pond, 1941.

They tended to 'coalesce' rhythmically in short snatches of their 'songs', especially when they used the same words; but tonally there was often little relationship. Then it was noticed that the younger child began to sing approximately the tonal configuration used by the elder child, but at a different pitch level. Gradually the tonal approximation became closer. One day the elder child, getting into a motor-car, started to chant:

(approximate pitch)

Ride   in   Dad-dy's   car—

The younger one joined in the chant at another pitch. The chant was repeated several times, as is quite usual when children seize on something that gives them pleasure. Eventually the pitch of the younger child coincided with the pitch of the older child, and from then on the two continued to chant in unison. This was the first time they had been observed singing together in unison. Subsequently they sang in unison more and more frequently, until unison singing became the usual occurrence. One would start a 'song', the other would join in at the same pitch. The leader was not always the elder child, but whoever was leader, the other child, when she wished to join in, would accommodate her pitch to that of the leader.

The foregoing illustration suggests that there are three developmental stages in response to melody: (1) rhythmic coalescence;[1] (2) grasp of the tonal configuration, more approximate than exact; and (3) coincidence[1] in pitch, when the

[1] The use of the terms 'coalesce' and 'coincide' is intentional, in order to suggest the difference in the way children 'come together' (*a*) rhythmically, and (*b*) tonally. 'Coalesce', derived from the Latin

exact tonal configuration is sung at the pitch of the stimulus tune.

The child seems to grasp the rhythmic pattern relatively easily, and in this he is helped by the rhythm of the words. The second and third stages appear to be closely associated, and pitch is involved in each. The intervals of the vocal response to the tonal shape of a melody tend to be only approximate until they coincide at the unison; then the vocal response corresponds in all respects with the tonal configuration of the stimulus tune.

Thus it would seem that, in response to melody, there is a strong urge towards coalescence upon a dominant rhythmic pattern, and a somewhat similar, but less strong, urge towards coincidence in pitch.

IMPORTANCE OF MEMORY

Coalescence upon a dominant rhythmic pattern and coincidence with a pitch pattern or tonal configuration are the result of the reactions of individuals to sound stimuli. However, these reactions are not simultaneous with the occurrence of the stimuli; the stimuli must come first. The child perceives, consciously or otherwise remembers what he has perceived, and then responds. He cannot participate at the very moment of the first hearing of the stimuli, since neither the rhythmic pulse upon which all rhythmic patterning depends nor the pitch pattern or tonal configuration is established. The

---

coalescere, suggests uniting in the sense of 'growing together'. 'Coincide', from the Latin *co-in*(*cidere* = *cadere*) suggests 'falling together', or 'happening upon' almost by chance, without necessarily fusing.

dominant 'pull' of a rhythmic stimulus cannot occur until regular pulse has been established and perceived; similarly with tonal configuration: the pitch pattern must be first established and perceived before it can exert a 'pull' towards coincidence with it. Then, but not before, is reaction possible. But by then the stimuli are no longer being heard for the first time, and memory has begun to play its part. Without the aid of memory no active participation in musical activity, however short, is possible.

In order to make accurate response to melody, a child must be able to perceive, and then retain in the memory for at least a short period of time, a given order of pitch intervals and note-lengths. These are the "heard sounds . . . possessing a meaningful relation to each other." When he can remember these in sufficient detail to identify a change in the melody, he has reached a stage of analysis. When such a change is in the tonal configuration of the melody, the pitch of at least one note has been changed, and judgments of pitch discrimination are involved.

3 Group-testing of Musical Ability

Advantages—Limitations—Disadvantages—Conditions

ADVANTAGES

The first obvious advantage of the group-test technique is that many more children can be tested within a limited time than by the individual-test method. When population trends of ability are sought the larger the number of subjects surveyed the clearer do those trends become. Conclusions drawn from a thousand samples are more convincing than conclusions based upon ten.

A further advantage of group-tests is that, by their very nature, they are constant for all subjects. In order to achieve this constancy good group-tests are so constructed that they are virtually self-administering; the instructions, examples, and the actual test material are the same for all subjects whether on the same or different occasions. The answers can only be right or wrong—*i.e.*, they are objective, and not dependent upon the subjective assessment of the marker.

There is also the advantage that group-tests may reveal

superior musical abilities in children who had previously given no indication of them. Such discovery of hitherto unsuspected ability may act as a motivator, and encourage a child to embark upon music-making to his personal satisfaction and self-fulfilment. There is, of course, no guarantee that such motivation will occur; the possession of superior abilities does not necessarily presuppose the desire to utilize them, but the probability is that it will do so.

LIMITATIONS

In one respect group-tests of musical ability are somewhat restrictive, since the circumstances of the testing prohibit any response in sound. The stimulus sounds are heard by all the subjects, but the subjects may respond only by writing their answers in silence. Otherwise, of course, audible responses would interfere with, and thus influence, the responses and answers of other subjects in the room.

However, this restriction upon overt audible response may not be such a disadvantage as might at first appear. It has already been stated that, in order to make an accurate vocal response to melody, a child must be able to perceive and then retain in the memory, for at least a short period of time, a given order of pitch intervals and note-lengths—*i.e.*, "heard sounds . . . possessing a meaningful relation to each other"— and that when he can remember these in sufficient detail to identify a change in the melody he has reached a stage of analysis.

Whatever the glandular and other reactions of the body may be to the stimulus of musical sounds, and however much the body and the mind may interact, in all but the most rudimentary reactions to music the mind is involved. Comparative and analytical judgments must be made. Judgments are mental processes, functions of the mind. Judgments control the necessary movements of the body in singing and in instrumental playing. Without these judgments no accurate control would be possible. They are a prerequisite of musical activity. Individual tests, in which audible responses are permissible, nevertheless require the judgments that control the audible responses. In fact, the latter are symptoms of the former.

In this respect, then, the conditions inherent in group-testing may not, after all, be a disadvantage. Restrictive they may be, but that to which they restrict their range of measurement—*i.e.*, the making of judgments upon the sound stimuli presented—is the very prerequisite of any progress in music-making. Musical ability is primarily a mental ability.

DISADVANTAGES

One decided disadvantage of group-test techniques is that they cannot be applied successfully to children who are not old enough, nor generally mature enough, to cope with the test situation. All subjects must be able clearly to understand from the recorded instructions, without further explanation, what they are required to do. They must already be able to write simple number or single-letter answers. They must be able to work in silence amongst other children doing likewise. They must be able to concentrate for at least the duration of a single test. In the investigation that will be described later it was found that the majority of children can cope with these conditions by the age of seven years, and that some of six years can also do this; but, in general, musical abilities cannot profitably be measured by means of group-tests before the age of seven years.

CONDITIONS

Group-tests, then, must be objective and uninfluenced by the person administering and marking them; their instructions must be in the simplest, clearest possible terms, so that they are intelligible to all subjects; they must also be valid—*i.e.*, they must be shown to measure that which they purport to measure, in this case some aspects of musical ability; they must be reliable—*i.e.*, they must show the same, or closely comparable, results if given to the same subjects on subsequent occasions. When young children are involved group-tests must not be so long as to overtax the powers of sustained concentration, or become tedious and so defeat their purpose. Here a balance has to be struck between the statistical desirability of a large number of items in each test and the child's restricted ability to remain interested in, and thus sustain concentration upon, numerous items requiring the same kind of mental operation. The short test battery has the added advantage that it can be completed within the normal Primary School lesson period, and so avoid disturbance to school organization. In practice this factor is not unimportant since the co-operation of head teachers and staff is essential, and the less their general organization is disrupted the more easily their willing co-operation is likely to be obtained.

4 Basic Musical Abilities and Reasons for Testing them

Memory—Distinction between tonal memory and rhythmic memory—Pitch discrimination—Chord analysis—Other abilities considered—No attempt to measure musical ability in toto; *Summary of basic assumptions underlying the tests selected*

MEMORY

The emergence of certain musical abilities in early years has already been described, and observation of these provides an indication as to what may profitably be measured.

It was seen that young children develop, as it were, melodically. Their early rhapsodic improvisations gradually become more organized as the memory develops until we find them repeating their own tunes or tunes they have heard from others. Initially their repetitions may be incomplete or inaccurate, but eventually they reach a stage of being able, un-prompted, to correct errors of detail. This implies keen memory for detail which involves analytical powers. These analytical powers seem to be well developed in children by the time they are mature enough to cope with the conditions of group-testing.

DISTINCTION BETWEEN TONAL MEMORY AND
RHYTHMIC MEMORY

Memory for melody, then, is an ability that develops at an early age; and this ability can be measured. When we come to devise the means of measuring this ability we recall that the two fundamental characteristics of melody that make one tune distinguishable from any other tune are the tonal and rhythmic aspects. We also note that the errors of detail that we find children spontaneously correcting in their performances are errors in both tonal configuration and in rhythm. The rhythmic aspect frequently seems to cause less trouble than the tonal; but when the rhythm is right children concentrate entirely for the moment on the tonal aspect. Similarly, when the tonal aspect is right they devote their whole attention to the rhythmic correction. They distinguish these two aspects, and deal with them separately.

This would seem to indicate that separate measurements should be made for these two essential and distinct aspects of memory for melody. Such a conclusion is supported by the evidence obtained from an earlier experiment[1] by the writer, in which a memory test was used that consisted of recognizably musical material—*i.e.*, actual melodies, or successions of pitch sounds within a rhythmic framework. The tonal and rhythmic elements were combined; some notes were long, some short. Subjects heard each melody twice and had to state whether the second playing was the same as the first or different. Whenever there was a difference in the second playing that difference was never more than a change of one note,

[1] See Chapter 5.

and this was a change in pitch; the rhythmic pattern remained constant, but the position in the melody of the changed note considerably affected the difficulty of judgment. If the change was on a long note, or on one that was rhythmically prominent, few errors were made; if it was on a note of the subdivided group of an unaccented pulse many errors were made.

PITCH DISCRIMINATION

Now the apperception of the tonal aspect of melody involves the ability to distinguish between different pitch sounds—*i.e.*, pitch discrimination. This ability is one that also appears to develop in the very early years; Seashore (1938) maintains that it is an innate talent. How finely is it necessary to be able to discriminate in pitch in order to take an effective part in music-making? No specific answer is available, although it is obvious that the keener the performer can discriminate the better.

There are two aspects to this question. In the first place we are concerned with the normally used pitch intervals of Occidental music: semitones, whole-tones, thirds, fifths, and so on. Do young children find some of these 'musical' intervals more difficult to discriminate than others? Do they reveal varying degrees of ability in making judgments upon the wide differences of pitch sounds comprising these intervals? The other aspect to the question concerns micro-intervals—*i.e.*, pitch differences smaller than the semitone. Although the semitone is the smallest 'musical' interval, the sounds involved form a relatively gross pitch difference. In addition to being able to distinguish between the 'musical' intervals, the performer must also be able to distinguish between the sounds of much smaller pitch differences in order to achieve unison, good intonation, and artistry.

Discussing this last point, Seashore (1938, p. 29), as a psychologist, states: "The medium of musical art lies primarily in artistic deviation from the fixed and regular"—*i.e.*, from rigid pitch, pulse, etc. Sir George Dyson (1954, pp. 78–79), as a musician, also discusses these deviations, and states that the normal field of expression is in the margin between "strict truth" and "caricature": "It is the mastery of such intuitive devices that gives an interpretation its distinction." In the early stages of music-making in groups our concern is to get the pupils singing or playing as nearly in tune as possible; otherwise the results are worse than Dyson's "caricature". For this purpose, as well as for subsequent possible "artistic deviation", keen pitch discrimination is essential.

What has not been established is precisely how keen pitch discrimination needs to be for practical music-making purposes. However, a test of pitch discrimination would reveal how finely children could in fact discriminate as well as measure different levels of this ability.

So far, then, we have found three basic musical abilities that we can attempt to measure in young children—tonal memory, rhythmic memory, and pitch discrimination—and it would appear that these three are indispensable in any musical operation.

CHORD ANALYSIS

One other type of judgment is also highly desirable in music-making: that of being aware of and being able to analyse concurrent sounds—*i.e.*, chord analysis. Whereas it is maintained that pitch discrimination and memory for tonal and rhythmic configurations are indispensable in any musical situation, an equally strong claim is not made for chord analysis. Hence the expression 'highly desirable'.

All the wind instruments, the strings, and certainly the voice, are concerned mainly with monophony—*i.e.*, one sound at a time. However, the historical development of music during the last thousand years, at any rate in the Western world, has been away from monophony towards polyphony and harmony. The singer usually performs to an accompaniment, or in company with others singing different parts; the instrumentalist, other than the keyboard player, is usually accompanied or is playing in ensemble, from duo, trio, or quartet up to full symphony orchestra. The individual may be making only one sound at a time, but his sound is usually one among many different concurrent sounds.

Appreciation of harmonic or polyphonic progression does not necessarily involve knowing the exact number of sounds heard at any given moment of time. Here it is rather the 'character' of the simultaneous combination of sounds, in terms of what has gone before and what will follow, that is important. Appreciation of harmony and polyphony depends upon and increases with experience.

The naming of the sounds heard in a chord depends upon training. The quality of chords—*e.g.*, concord, discord—is a more mature concept. The older candidate in a music examination might describe a chord—*e.g.*, first inversion of the dominant seventh—without knowing the exact number of sounds heard, which indeed might be four, five, or more if doubling at the octave is admitted. But if no notes are doubled —*i.e.*, if all the notes of the chord are different—he must be able to hear all those notes in order to name the chord correctly. In order to sing back to the examiner any one or all of these notes—a common examination task—he must also be able to hear all of them. If he can hear all the constituent notes of the chord clearly enough to sing them he can perform the very elementary operation of counting the number of such notes as he hears.

A chord test of some kind is a common ingredient of music examinations. Wing (1948, pp. 14–15) discusses this, and he includes a test of chord analysis in his battery of tests. His subjects are "merely asked to state the number of notes." This was "in order to adapt the test on chord analysis so that it would be suitable as a group test which would not involve acquired knowledge." Revesz (1953, p. 110) also used a test of chord analysis as a measure of musical ability, giving the following reason for this:

> The analysis and identification of the constituent notes of a chord is one of the problems of the musical ear. . . . That analysis and the discrimination of component notes does not depend in the main on musical training, but chiefly on the inherent musical talent, is attested by the fact that musically disposed children, even before their first musical instruction, are able to analyse dissonant triads and tetrads with great ease.

What degree of 'musical disposition' children must possess in order to be able to "analyse dissonant triads and tetrads with great ease" has not been established. A generally held opinion is that very young children do not pay much attention to the accompaniments of their melodies. Whether or not the harmonization is appropriate, in the sense accepted by the musician, does not appear to worry them; the chordal 'background' to their all-important tunes is relatively unimportant.

Only sparse evidence exists to indicate when children begin to take an interest in the chordal 'background' to melody, and when they can analyse the tonal ingredients of concurrent sounds. Yet the ability to analyse groups of two, three, four, or possibly more, concurrent sounds is important in music-practice; and a test of this ability would prove a useful addition to the tests of pitch discrimination, tonal memory, and rhythmic memory already proposed.

In answer to the question, what exactly is to be measured? we have now proposed three abilities as basic, elemental, and essential for music-making: tonal memory, rhythmic memory, and pitch discrimination. We have added, as highly desirable, the ability to analyse chords.

OTHER ABILITIES CONSIDERED

Are there other abilities as fundamental as these? Timbre and loudness have already been dealt with (Chapter 2, p. 24, above). Tests of aesthetic aspects of musical enjoyment or taste, such as Wing's tests of appropriateness of rhythmic accent, harmony, intensity, and phrasing (Wing 1947), involve maturer concepts, and are outside the scope of group-tests for the very young because of relative lack of musical experience. However desirable it might be to use such additional tests with older subjects, it may be reasonably maintained that they do not measure the absolutely basic, elemental abilities which are already apparent amongst children at an early age, and without which any success in music-making would be impossible.

We are left, then, with the abilities of pitch discrimination, tonal memory, rhythmic memory, and chord analysis. It now remains to describe how tests to measure these abilities were constructed, and to state the results of their application to young children.

NO ATTEMPT TO MEASURE MUSICAL ABILITY IN TOTO —SUMMARY OF BASIC ASSUMPTIONS UNDERLYING THE TESTS SELECTED

However, before we do this it might be well to remind ourselves that we are not attempting to measure musical ability *in toto*, but only some aspects of it. It might also be well to summarize the assumptions upon which the tests are based. These are:

(1) that the most elemental form of music is the melodic phrase or figure, which comprises tonal configuration within a rhythmic framework;

(2) that apprehension of melody is impossible without the ability to recall, in detail, sounds that have already been heard, and this depends upon the ability to apprehend the constituent factors of melody—*i.e.*, pitch and time;

(3) that finer-than-semitone pitch discrimination is essential in singing and all instrumental playing, except at the keyboard, in order to achieve the necessary good intonation;

(4) that, whereas concurrent sounds (chords) are not fundamental to melody, it is necessary for the singer or monophonic instrumentalist to be aware of the different sounds of other singers or instru-

mentalists in performance, and that the greater his awareness the more appropriate his own contribution to the ensemble is likely to be.

We must also first give an account of an earlier experiment, the results of which influenced the construction of the subsequent tests, and are also of interest in themselves.

5 Pilot Tests of Memory and Pitch Discrimination

Need for specially devised tests—Description of the pilot tests—Some information about the children who worked the tests—Results of the testing—Discussion of the results

NEED FOR SPECIALLY DEVISED TESTS

No previously published group-test had been devised *primarily* for the younger children. Some of the published tests—for example, those of Kwalwasser (1927), Seashore (1939), and Wing (1947)—have subsequently been used with younger children, but they were originally devised for, and standardized upon, older children. For instance, Seashore (1939) states that his "Measures" "may be used first in the fifth grade"—that is, not before the age of ten or eleven years. Anastasi (1954, p. 437) maintains: "The Seashore tests are applicable from the fifth grade to the adult level. The testing of younger children by this procedure has not proved feasible because of the difficulty of sustaining interest and attention." Wing, in the leaflet of information and guidance accompanying his tests, states: "The tests [*i.e.*, the Wing Tests] are suitable for group application . . . for ten years [of age] or so, and above." At a later date Wing (1956, p. 33) adds that his "own interest was directed to this particular field because of the practical need to select those children who *at the age of eleven* might profitably take up the study of an orchestral instrument."

Tests primarily devised for older children may or may not be appropriate for sorting out children several years younger. They might, for example, omit an ability which it is desired to measure: for instance, the Wing battery contains no test of finer-than-semitone pitch discrimination; on the other hand, they might measure certain abilities which depend upon greater maturity and experience and/or training than are to be found amongst the very young. Furthermore, the method of measurement of a specific ability may be quite appropriate for the maturer subject, but too complicated and confusing for the younger child; an example of this will be seen when our first memory test is discussed later in this chapter.

Standardized group-tests in other spheres—*e.g.*, intelligence tests and attainment tests—are constructed with definite age groups in mind, and their standards of difficulty and their methods are based upon keen observation of, and experience with, children of those age groups, as well as upon the hypotheses adopted by the test-constructor. Similarly with group-tests of musical ability; they, equally, must be devised for the age groups of children whom it is desired to test, and be based upon the results of observation of, and experience with, children of those age groups.

It was with such considerations as these in mind that the writer decided to set about the task of trying to find the means of measuring abilities that observation and experience indicated were already apparent in younger children. Such abilities were, in the first place, memory and pitch discrimination; and tests to measure these were constructed.[1]

DESCRIPTION OF THE PILOT TESTS

1. *Memory Test*

The memory test consisted of thirty pairs of tunes, played on the pianoforte, ranging in length from three notes to ten. Wing's published memory test (1947) was used as a model, but a change was made in the type of judgment required. Wing requires his subjects to locate the exact place in each melody where a change is made in the second playing. This involves counting the sounds as they are heard, and either recording a numerical figure or locating one of a printed line of dots corresponding to the number of sounds in each item. It was felt that this element of counting, particularly beyond the span of digits of one hand in the items with more than five sounds, might be a distraction for young children. Therefore they were asked to state merely whether the second tune of each pair was the same as or different from the first, recording as answer either 'S' or 'D'. This involved the making of some of the items 'same', whereas all the Wing memory test items are different. Of the thirty pairs of tunes, eight were 'same' and twenty-two 'different'. In the latter case not more than one sound was altered, and this was always a difference in pitch, and never a difference in note-length; thus the rhythm in the second tune of each pair was always the same as the rhythm of the first tune.

[1] A more detailed account may be read in the author's unpublished thesis (Bentley, 1963).

The second tune of each pair was played as nearly like the first as is possible, except, of course, for the changed note in each of the 'different' items. Every effort was made to maintain the same tempo, note-lengths, phrasing, and dynamics, and to avoid accenting the changed note.

Prepared instructions were first read aloud, and one example of a 'same' item and one of a 'different' item was given, together with the correct answers.

2. *Pitch Discrimination Test*

In the pitch discrimination test thirty pairs of pitch sounds were played on the pianoforte, each sound being sustained for approximately one second. The second sound of each pair followed immediately after the first. The answers involved the writing of a single letter: 'S' for 'same', if the second sound of a pair was the same as the first; 'U' for 'up' and 'D' for 'down', where pitch movement between the two notes of a pair was involved. The terms 'up' and 'down' were chosen as being more suggestive of movement than 'higher' and 'lower'.

Prepared instructions were first read aloud to the group, and these were followed by one example of each kind of item— 'same', 'up', and 'down'—together with the correct answers.

The aim of this test was to discover if the size of the interval —*i.e.*, the pitch difference—affected the difficulty of making pitch discrimination judgments. At this stage only 'musical' intervals were used—*i.e.*, no smaller pitch differences than those involved in the semitone, the smallest interval normally used in Occidental music. Thus, in addition to a few unison ('same') items, intervals from the semitone to the minor tenth were included, employing all the semitonal steps occurring

M.A.C.–D

within the range: A below middle C to E two octaves and a third above middle C.

Copies of the instructions and of the notation of the items of the memory and pitch discrimination tests may be seen at the end of this chapter.

SOME INFORMATION ABOUT THE CHILDREN WHO WORKED THE TESTS

The two pilot tests of memory and pitch discrimination were used in ordinary Local Education Authority Primary Schools, with classes of nine- to eleven-year-old children. It was considered that, by the age of nine years, children generally would be quite mature enough to cope with this novel group-test situation; that the majority would have formed, from day-to-day experience, concepts of 'same' and 'different', 'up' and 'down', in reference to pitch; that they would find no difficulty with the actual operation of writing the simple answers required; and that they would not be likely to experience undue fatigue in completing the short tests. Furthermore, at this age children usually give enthusiastic and unselfconscious co-operation in a new kind of experience.

Three hundred and twelve children worked the tests: 142 boys and 170 girls. As measured by Moray House Verbal Reasoning Tests their I.Q.s ranged from 75 to 140+; the mean I.Q. was 103; and the distribution of I.Q.s was normal.[1]

RESULTS OF THE TESTING
Memory Test

The scores ranged from 7 to 30 (the maximum); the mean score was 19; the distribution of the scores was normal.[1]

[1] See Chapter 7, p. 86, footnote.

There was no significant difference between the scores of boys and girls. Correlation[1] between I.Q.s and test scores was as low as 0·2 and barely significant. Reliability[2] on re-test was 0·6 and significant.

Analysis of the results showed that the difficulty of judgment on any single item of the thirty was influenced by at least four factors:

    (1) The length of the item. In general the longer items proved more difficult than the shorter, but not consistently so throughout the note-groupings from three-note to ten-note tunes.

    (2) The relative length, and therefore rhythmic prominence, of the changed note. For items in which the changed note was one of a whole-pulse the mean error was 38 per cent; for items in which the changed note was shorter than a whole-pulse the mean error was 52 per cent.

    (3) The serial position in the tune of the changed note. Changes on the first and last notes produced a mean error of 24 per cent; changes on intermediate notes produced a mean error of 52 per cent.

    (4) The size of the pitch interval of the changed note. The mean error for items involving a change of a whole-tone was 34 per cent; that for items involving a change of a semitone was 52 per cent.

The interaction of these four factors in all the items apparently caused confusion. For instance, judgments upon the

[1] See Chapter 7, p. 87, footnote 1.
[2] See Chapter 7, p. 88.

tonal aspects of the melodies was confused by the rhythmic features. Furthermore, in discussion with the children after the tests, it became evident that some had been distracted by the large number of notes in the items towards the end of the test, and, as a result, had merely made vague guesses; others said that they had tried to count the notes as they were heard (although they had not been asked to do this), so that they would know when to expect the end of the second tune of each pair. Apparently, the differing lengths of the items further contributed towards confusion.

All this seemed to indicate that, in measuring memory, the tonal and rhythmic elements should be separated, and that all the items should be of constant length.

Pitch Discrimination Test

The scores ranged from 7 to 30 (the maximum); the mean score was 24; the distribution of the scores was non-normal.

The size of the pitch interval affected the difficulty of judgment. The mean correct score for each of the different intervals used is shown in Table I.

TABLE I. PITCH DISCRIMINATION—MEAN CORRECT SCORES FOR SEMITONES AND LARGER INTERVALS

Size of pitch interval difference	Mean item correct score
Semitone	60 per cent
Whole-tone	77 per cent
Major and minor thirds	77 per cent
Perfect fifth	83 per cent
Larger intervals	91 per cent
Unison	92 per cent

It is seen that the most difficult items, the semitones, were judged correctly by 60 per cent of the subjects, that the whole-tone and the thirds were judged correctly by 77 per cent, the fifth by 83 per cent, and the rest of the larger intervals by over 90 per cent. These scores, considered also in conjunction with the fact that more children achieved 29/30 than any other scores, indicate that this test was too easy: some 15 per cent of the children scored 30—*i.e.*, full marks—and 90 per cent scored over half-marks. Such a test would not sufficiently challenge the abilities of the more able children.

The evidence indicates that the larger intervals are easier to discriminate than the smaller, but it also suggests that young children might be able to judge much smaller pitch differences than those involved in the semitone.

There was no significant difference between the scores of boys and girls. As far as could be ascertained, intelligence had little influence on the test scores, and the test was reliable.

DISCUSSION OF THE RESULTS

The pilot tests provided some information about the abilities of children in memory and pitch discrimination. They had, however, themselves been on test, and had revealed certain limitations indicating the need for considerable revision before they could profitably be used as measures of ability on a wider age range of children.

The first of these limitations is concerned with constancy in administration. It will have been realized that these two tests were not recorded, but played on the pianoforte in the class-room by the test administrator, who also read aloud the instructions and gave the examples. The original intention had been to devise very simply administered tests that might be given by a class-teacher with the minimum of apparatus—namely, a sheet of instructions to be read to the subjects by the teacher, and a music-notation score of the test items to be played by the teacher on the pianoforte, the instrument to which young children in school are usually most accustomed. It had been observed that some teachers had attempted to make the Wing tests more personal and intimate by playing the items, or their own versions of them, on the pianoforte instead of by means of the gramophone records. This had then led to their playing only some of the Wing test items; which, of course, completely invalidates the standardized scores. By the making of both the instructions and the actual items of the present tests extremely simple and short it had been hoped to provide the teacher who prefers to play the items himself with a tool which would be easily accessible, easy to administer, and with which he might be less tempted to interfere. However, as will be seen, this hope had to be abandoned.

Even when administered by one person only, and that person exercising the greatest care in both the reading of the instructions and in the playing of the test material, the tests could not be entirely constant as between different groups of subjects on different occasions; administered by different people they would be even less so. Therefore it was decided that the instructions, examples, and the test items must be recorded, on tape or disc, in order to eliminate the temptation to interfere and other causes of lack of constancy in administration.

Another limitation was in the content of the tests themselves. The memory test had consisted of recognizably 'musical' material—*i.e.*, the tonal and rhythmic elements had been combined, as is normal in melody. However, analysis of the results had revealed at least four different factors affecting the difficulty of an item, and this had led to confusion. Therefore the decision was taken to measure the tonal and rhythmic aspects of memory separately. This decision has the support of some other investigators. For instance, Spearman (1927, p. 340) found that "the abilities to appreciate the relations of pitch . . . and rhythm have extremely low correlation"; and Henkin (1957, p. 305): "The melodic and rhythmic factors are shown to be independent mathematically and psychologically." Moreover, in practice, teachers and conductors are well aware that, in the process of learning, it is sometimes necessary to separate the tonal and rhythmic aspects of a passage or figure; and one department of music-making— namely, percussion playing—is primarily if not exclusively concerned with the rhythmic aspect alone.

Furthermore, in view of the additional confusion arising from changing the lengths of the items, it was decided that all the items should be of the same length. By separating the tonal and rhythmic aspects, and, in addition, by making all the items of the same length, each limited to the number of sounds that could be counted on the digits of one hand, the tests of memory could be made more critical by introducing the element of locating the exact position in the melody of a tonal change, or the exact position in the pattern of a rhythmic change. This would involve more specific analysis than was required in the perception of an unspecified change in the melody as a whole, and would require keener concentration and attention to detail. It would become a more critical test of memory in so far as the first tune or pattern of each pair must be remembered completely accurately in order to locate the exact position of a change in the second presentation. Such a test would also be more reliable statistically, since more answers would be available for each item than the previous alternatives of 'same' or 'different'.

The pitch discrimination test had revealed that larger intervals are easier for young children to judge than smaller intervals, but that even the smallest interval of a semitone was judged correctly by 60 per cent of the subjects. The test was too easy, and in any case it did not provide a measure of the child's ability to make the finer pitch discrimination judgments that are necessary for good intonation, and which have already been discussed in Chapter 4. It was therefore decided to make a new pitch discrimination test in which the pitch differences would be gradually reduced from the semitone. From the pilot test a certain amount of information had been obtained about children's judgments on 'musical' intervals, of which the semitone had been the smallest; now the semitone would be the largest interval or pitch difference. Obviously neither the pianoforte nor any other keyboard instrument would be able to produce the necessary sounds for the items of the new test, and other means must be found.

The preliminary work had now been done to point the way towards the measurement of the three basic musical abilities discussed in Chapter 4—namely, tonal memory, rhythmic memory, and pitch discrimination. Whilst new tests of these abilities were being constructed it was decided to add a further test of that "other type of judgment that is also highly desirable in music-making"—namely, chord analysis.

Pilot Pitch Discrimination Test

"Two notes will be played; sometimes the second note is the same as the first: then you will write 'S' for 'same'; sometimes the second note goes up: then you will write 'U' for 'up'; sometimes the second note goes down: then you will write 'D' for 'down'. Is that clear? 'S' for 'same', 'U' for 'up', 'D' for 'down'. If you are not quite sure, write the answer you think may be correct. I shall call out each number as we come to it."

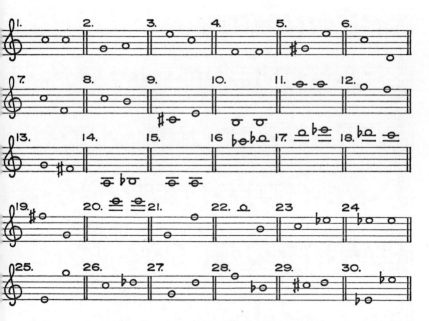

Pilot Memory Test

"Thirty tunes will each be played twice; sometimes the second playing will be the same as the first: then you will write

'S' for 'same'; sometimes in the second playing one note will be altered, and so it will be different from the first: then you will write 'D' for 'different'. If you are not quite sure, write the answer you think may be correct. I shall call out each number as we come to it."

6 *Development of the New Test Battery*

Pitch discrimination test—Memory tests, tonal and rhythmic—Chord analysis test—Recording and reproduction—Instructions and examples—The answer form—Order of presentation of the tests—Administration of the battery—Texts of the instructions for the tests

The new test battery was developed through several versions, all of which were tried out on large numbers of children. In the light of data obtained at each stage of development, modifications were made in the content of the tests, in the instructions, in the means of creating the sounds, and in the answer forms. Four tests were eventually devised: pitch discrimination, tonal memory, rhythmic memory, and chord analysis. All the tests, complete with instructions and examples, were recorded, so that they are virtually self-administering and require no further explanation or interpretation by the administrator. A description of each test follows, together with a brief account of its development.

PITCH DISCRIMINATION TEST

In Chapter 5 it was seen that the smallest interval used in the pilot test, the semitone, was judged accurately by 60 per cent of the subjects, even though it was heard in contrast with larger intervals and, therefore, by comparison was the smallest and most difficult. In the new test the semitone became the biggest pitch difference, and smaller-than-semitone differences had to be created. Since normal musical instruments could not produce the accurately measured pitch differences required, specially calibrated sine-wave oscillators were used to create the sounds. These sounds were then recorded on tape.

The note A = 440 cycles per second (*i.e.*, the note in the second space of the treble clef) was taken as the starting-point, and all the pitch differences were measured from this. The reasons for making A = 440 c.p.s. the reference tone were as follows. This pitch sound is approximately in the middle of the pitch range of a young child's voice, and it has been maintained that the larynx assists pitch discrimination even when no conscious vocal response is made by the listener. For instance, Vernon (1932, p. 67) states: "Undoubtedly the larynx or vocal cords are of great importance in the recognition of pitch change." If indeed this is the case, then it would seem that the sounds of pitch differences within the vocal range would be easier to discriminate than sounds outside the vocal range.

There was evidence that this might be so in the data obtained from an earlier version of the pitch discrimination test, where the first six items were differences of a semitone: items 1 and 2 started from A = 440 c.p.s.; items 3 and 4 started from A = 880 c.p.s. (*i.e.*, an octave higher, and just outside the child's easy vocal range); and items 5 and 6 started from A = 220 c.p.s. (*i.e.*, an octave lower, and also just outside the child's easy vocal range). The errors recorded on these three registers were as follows:

440 c.p.s.	880 c.p.s.	220 c.p.s.
8 per cent	20 per cent	19 per cent

We see that there is virtually no difference in difficulty between the higher and lower octave, but each of these is considerably more difficult than the register in the middle of the vocal range.

In the final version of the pitch discrimination test all the items are based upon A = 440 c.p.s. as the reference tone. The first two items consist of semitone steps (*i.e.*, differences of 26 c.p.s. at this pitch level); one item moves up, the other down, as is the case with the remaining smaller pitch differences of the test. The next two items are differences of 18 c.p.s. (*i.e.*, about three-quarters of a semitone), and the next are differences of 12 c.p.s. Now a difference of 12 c.p.s. is approximately half a semitone at this pitch level. Pitch differences of half a semitone or greater are easier to judge correctly than smaller differences; the latter, although there is actually a difference, are frequently judged as 'same'. Therefore, in order to provide a more secure basis of comparison, a 'same' item (*i.e.*, an item containing two sounds of exactly the same pitch) is introduced between the 10 c.p.s. and 8 c.p.s. pitch differences, and another between the 5 c.p.s. and 4 c.p.s. pitch differences. These 'tonal anchors' assist subjects in detecting differences when they actually occur in subsequent items. The pitch differences used in the test are shown in Table II (p. 76).

The second sound of each pair is presented immediately after the first, and each sound is sustained for one second. Between the cessation of the second sound of an item and the announcement of the number of the next item six seconds are allowed to elapse. Subjects are asked to state if the second sound of each pair is the same as the first (answer: 'S') or if it moves up or down (answer: 'U' or 'D').

In an earlier experimental version of the pitch discrimination test, differences of 2 c.p.s. and 1 c.p.s. had been included. These are differences of approximately one-thirteenth and one-twenty-sixth of a semitone. Analysis of the scores and errors recorded on these smallest differences indicated that the answers were unreliable and to some extent the result of guessing. This may be due to subjective difficulties intrinsic in making judgments upon such small pitch differences, but it may also be due to the physical circumstances of recording and playing back the sounds through a loudspeaker. At this level of pitch difference merely moving the head whilst a sustained sound is heard can suggest a slight change of pitch. This may be attributed to properties of the ear. However, there is the further complication that recording and play-back equipment may not be absolutely perfect. Owing to induced harmonics or overtones caused by resonance in the amplifiers and speakers, the pure tones of the oscillator creating the original sounds may cease to be pure, with a consequent change in the timbre of the sound heard; and at the level of these smallest differences a change of timbre, in itself, could suggest a slight rise or fall in pitch.

Therefore, in view of the difficulties intrinsic in the subjective judgment of such small pitch differences, and those involved in the recording and reproduction of the sounds, it appeared that the smallest useful pitch difference in a group-test for use in the school classroom via a loudspeaker need not be less than a difference of 3 c.p.s. If circumstances were to arise where measurement of even smaller differences was considered desirable, it could be more reliably accomplished with individual subjects in a laboratory, where all the external factors could be brought under more critical control.

MEMORY TESTS

Experience with the pilot test of memory had indicated that the tonal and rhythmic aspects of memory should be measured separately, that all the items should be of the same length, and that answers should require the exact location of any change in the second presentation of an item. Accordingly, separate tests of tonal memory and of rhythmic memory were devised.

Tonal Memory Test

The new tonal memory test consists of ten items of paired comparisons, each half of each item being a five-note tune. In the second half of each item one note is changed by either a whole-tone or a semitone. The pitch range is restricted to sounds well within the easy vocal range of young children: note D below the bottom line of the treble clef to note A a perfect fifth above. All the notes are of equal length, and there are no dynamic accents; thus there are no rhythmic complications. The speed of playing is about 120 notes to the minute. The positions of the changed notes are equally but randomly distributed between the first and the fifth. There are five changes of a semitone and five of a whole-tone, one each for each serial-position change. Between the cessation of the last sound of an item and the announcement of the number of the next item six seconds elapse.

Subjects are asked to state if the second playing of each pair is the same as the first, or, if there is a change, to state the position of the altered note. None of the items is, in fact, the 'same', but subjects who do not recognize a difference should have the opportunity of stating this.

The sounds of the final version of the tonal memory test were played on a pipe organ, on eight-foot and four-foot flute stops.

Rhythmic Memory Test

The new rhythmic memory test also consists of ten items of paired comparisons, each half of each item being a four-pulse rhythmic figure. The speed of playing is about 72 pulses to the minute. Between the cessation of the last sound of an item and the announcement of the number of the next item six seconds elapse. The recordings were made from a pipe organ, using eight-foot small diapason and two-foot fifteenth stops.

Subjects are asked to state whether the second half of each item is the 'same' as the first, or, if 'different', to state the pulse on which the change is made. Thus five possible answers are available: S 1 2 3 4. Eight items contain a change in the second half. Two items do not, and the second half of each of these two items is a re-recording of the first half, since it is virtually impossible to play the same pattern twice in exactly the same way in respect of absolute note-lengths.

Since this is a test of rhythmic memory, as distinct from tonal memory, there is no change of pitch within each item; the eight pulses of the first and second parts of each item are played on the same note. However, in order to avoid the monotony of hearing all ten items of the test on one note, the pitch of each item is changed.

The positions of the changed pulses are equally but randomly distributed between the first and the fourth. Changes on the last—*i.e.*, the fourth—pulse might be criticized on the grounds that the quicker figures of divided pulses should, musically, lead on to longer notes. In order to meet such criticism, it would have been possible to add a fifth pulse to each item; however, this would have increased the length of an already long test and complicated the instructions. Alternatively, the number of possible answers could have been reduced, by retaining four pulses but making the last sound in all items a single-pulse note, and thus not changeable in the second part of an item. If the length of the test was not to be increased, and if no fewer than five possible answers were to be retained, which was desirable from the point of view of reliability, at least two items must have a change on the last pulse.

CHORD ANALYSIS TEST

Much experiment was necessary before a satisfactory version of the chord analysis test was achieved. The problems to be solved were twofold: (i) in the actual content of the chords and (ii) in the recording and reproduction. To some extent these overlapped, but we shall consider them separately.

In the first place, it was not known how many notes,

sounded simultaneously, young children could be expected to distinguish. Revesz (1953, p. 151, and 1925, pp. 74–83), whilst investigating the abilities of a young musical prodigy, found that at seven years of age the boy could analyse, "absolutely correctly", chords containing as many as seven different notes. However, our concern is not with child prodigies, except possibly by some very remote chance, but with normal children. If an individual is discovered to possess abilities far in excess of the normal range for his age he may then be given more searching tests. Merely by revealing hitherto unsuspected potential the group-test satisfactorily accomplishes one of its functions. The follow-up on any such discovery must involve individual testing techniques.

In an early version of this test five-note chords were used, in addition to two-, three-, and four-note chords. Examination of the answers revealed that some children had answered correctly on the five-note chords whilst giving incorrect answers for two- and three-note chords. Since chords containing many notes are intrinsically more difficult to analyse than chords with few notes, the obvious conclusion was that some of these correct answers were the result of lucky guesses. This conclusion was confirmed by the fact that others, who scored well on the two- and three-note chords, more often made mistakes on the four-note and five-note chords; and by the additional fact that, on re-test, the statistical reliability[1] of this early version of the test was unsatisfactory $(r = 0.21)$.

Therefore a new test was constructed containing thirty items: eleven two-note chords including every interval from

[1] See Chapter 7, p. 88.

the minor second to the major seventh, twelve three-note chords, and seven four-note chords. All the notes used were within the vocal range of young children. From these thirty items twenty were to be selected.

This thirty-item test was given twice to seventy-six boys and girls aged nine to eleven years, and the order of difficulty of the chords was established. The mean score for both applications of the test was below 50 per cent correct (first trial 13/30; second trial 14/30). In view of this, and of the age of the children, which was rather higher than that of many who would eventually be tested, it seemed reasonable that, in selecting the twenty chords for the new test, the ten most difficult of the thirty items should be eliminated. These ten most difficult items were five four-note chords, four three-note chords, and one two-note chord (the major third, which had proved to be the next-to-most-difficult item: 68 per cent errors, and nearly all of these stating 3 notes).

The new twenty-item test now consisted of ten two-note chords, eight three-note chords, and two four-note chords. This was given twice to other groups of children of the same age range as the earlier group. The statistical reliability[1] improved ($r = 0.69$), which suggests that the answers were less subject to guessing than formerly; and the group-item mean correct scores were as follows:

Two-note chords	*Three-note chords*	*Four-note chords*
64 per cent	54 per cent	44 per cent

This discovered order of difficulty is what one could reason-

[1] See Chapter 7, p. 88.

ably expect, and it was confirmed on subsequent occasions: the fewer the notes, the easier the chord is to analyse.

It will be appreciated that, unlike the pitch discrimination test, the items of the chord analysis test cannot be presented in the strict order of easy-to-difficult. Such a procedure would result in a pattern of answers that an intelligent child might quickly discover. For instance, in the order of easy-to-difficult, the figure '2' would be the correct answer for eight out of the first nine items. Therefore, after a relatively easy start, the two-, three-, and four-note items are presented in such an order that it would be difficult to discover any pattern in the answers.

The new chord analysis test, then, consists of twenty items of two-, three-, and four-note chords. No two adjacent items have any one note in common; the reason for this is that the repetition of a note in adjacent chords might give undue prominence to that note, induce a feeling for tonality as a result, and thus possibly confuse the judgment of the subject. All the notes of all the items lie within the vocal range of young children.

Each chord is sounded for three seconds. Although children working the tests are requested not to make any sound, occasional coughs or shuffles are inevitable. In practice, however, it has been found that such interruptions are usually quite short, and that, in the space of three seconds, there is plenty of time left clearly to hear again the sounds of the chord interrupted. Between the cessation of the chord of one item and the announcement of the number of the next item six seconds elapse. Subjects are asked to state the number of sounds they hear in each chord.

RECORDING AND REPRODUCTION

The means of creating and recording the sounds of the pitch discrimination, tonal memory, and rhythmic memory tests have already been described. The problems involved in the making of the chord analysis test were much more difficult to solve. In the earlier versions the chords had been played on the pianoforte and recorded on tape. The pianoforte has the advantage of being the instrument to which most children are likely to be accustomed. However, its disadvantages outweigh this advantage of familiarity. In the first place, it is extremely difficult to play all the notes of a chord equally loudly; and if one note is played less loudly than the rest it will be partially masked by the other notes. Secondly, the initial relatively loud clang is followed by an immediate and rapid decrease in loudness, even within the limits of three seconds duration. This also causes especial difficulty in recording, since, if the recording level is set high enough for the later part of the sustained chord to be audible, the initial clang causes distortion.

Therefore, in further attempts to improve the quality of the sounds, and of the recording, three different pipe organs were used, but these also proved inadequate. In addition to the required sounds, the microphone also registered other unwanted sounds: from the resonance of the building, from the blowing apparatus (which normally was not noticed), and even from the 'plop' of the key-to-pipe action. Furthermore, slight sluggishness in the key-to-pipe action resulted in some notes of a chord being sounded slightly longer than others, thus giving such notes undue prominence. Such minor defects are not particularly noticeable when the organs are in normal use;

but for the making of the sounds for the chord analysis test the instruments available did not come up to the necessary standard. In any case, apart from the shortcomings of the instruments themselves, there were always the acoustical properties of the buildings to be reckoned with.

Next, the chords were played on an electronic organ, and the recording was also made electronically—*i.e.*, by direct line from the amplifiers of the organ to those of the tape-recorder. By this means unwanted external sounds, such as would inevitably be picked up by a microphone in acoustical recording, were eliminated. However, this means of recording created a new problem. Now resultant-notes (sub-harmonics) were heard, not very loudly but sufficiently so to be distracting to expert adult listeners. Furthermore, the prominence of these resultant-notes varied according to the loudspeaker used in play-back: a large speaker with a strong bass response emphasized them more than a small speaker with a weaker bass response. Since the tests would be played on a variety of record-players it was important that these resultant-notes should be eliminated.

Another attempt was made to create the sounds by means of sine-wave oscillators. The original sounds, as checked by instruments in the laboratory, and judged subjectively, were clear and free from resultant-notes and other defects. The recordings were not.

Therefore, resort was made yet again to a pipe organ, but this time it was possible to make the recording under better conditions than formerly when pipe organs had been used. The chords were played on an eight-foot open diapason stop, which was the rank of pipes giving the clearest sounds, as judged subjectively in the building and on listening to the recording.

In a group-test, which must be constant in all respects as between the different groups to whom it is given, the instructions and examples play an important part. They must be such that they will be clearly intelligible to all subjects, and comprehensive, yet not so long as to tax unduly the powers of concentration of even the youngest subject.

The instructions and examples for the new tests were discussed with class teachers, and tried out on a number of seven- and eight-year-old children of wide general ability range. Modifications were made until it was quite clear that the instructions were neither likely to be misunderstood, nor so long as to become tedious and thus cause loss of attention. Young children follow the latest version of the instructions and examples with ease, and often show satisfaction, sometimes almost amounting to glee, when the loud-speaker announces an obviously correct answer in the examples.

THE ANSWER FORM

In one of the earlier versions of the tests the instructions were printed on the answer form as well as spoken on the tape. However, when this answer form was used it was suspected that some of the less fluent readers found the printed instructions confusing. Therefore a check was made with classes of eight- and nine-year-old boys and girls upon the relative ease of intelligibility of the instructions, on the one hand when they were listened to without the printed form, and on the other hand when reading and listening were concurrent. All the children could read, with varying degrees of fluency. Some children were told to read the instructions at the same time as they were being heard from the loud-speaker; other children, of comparable reading ability, merely listened. Subsequent questioning indicated that those children who had merely listened understood more clearly than those who had been asked to listen and read at the same time. Of the latter, some had been ahead of the spoken word in their reading, others had lagged behind. From then on printed instructions were omitted from the answer forms.

The titles of the four tests were also made as simple as possible both in the spoken instructions and on the answer form. The pitch discrimination test is referred to simply as 'Pitch'; the tonal memory and rhythmic memory tests are respectively called 'Tunes' and 'Rhythm'; and the chord analysis test 'Chords'. Thus all likely causes of confusion or distraction have been removed, as have also all pretexts for test administrators to interpret the instructions, or otherwise interfere with them.

ORDER OF PRESENTATION OF THE TESTS

The test battery is in three parts: pitch discrimination, memory, and chord analysis. Each part contains twenty items. Memory is divided into tonal memory and rhythmic memory, each with ten items. The total number of items in the battery is sixty.

In the presentation of the tests, pitch discrimination comes first. Experience has shown this to be a good test to start with. The instructions are simple; the early items are easy; superior smiles have been noticed on the faces of some children when they found these early items of the battery so easy, smiles that gradually faded, however, as concentration upon the ever-smaller pitch differences increased!

Tonal memory is presented next. In this test the kind of judgment required is quite different from that needed for the pitch discrimination test. Here the subjects must count five notes as they are played, and recognize exactly where a change occurs in the second playing of each item. The rhythmic memory test requires a comparable kind of judgment, but now counting four pulses instead of five pitch sounds. Each of these tests of memory, although containing only ten items, occupies about as much time as the pitch discrimination test, and as the chord analysis test. If the rhythmic memory test followed straight on after the tonal memory test a similar kind of judgment would be required for a period of some ten minutes. Therefore, in order to give variety, the chord analysis test, which lasts some five minutes, and which requires a quite different kind of judgment, is inserted between the two tests of memory.

Thus we have the four tests presented in the order of:

> pitch discrimination
> tonal memory
> chord analysis
> rhythmic memory

Each lasts between four and a half and five and a half minutes, and the whole battery takes about twenty minutes to complete. The whole operation, including filling in the particulars at the head of the answer form, can be completed in less than half an hour.

ADMINISTRATION OF THE BATTERY

Experience has shown that children even as young as seven years of age can complete the whole battery in one session without showing signs of fatigue. However, it is not essential that all four tests be given at the same time. If they are not so given it is suggested that the marking of the completed tests be deferred until the whole battery has been presented, so that children are not aware of their scores in the earlier tests when completing the rest. If this were to happen children with low scores in the earlier tests might, on seeing them, become discouraged, and so not do themselves justice in the remaining tests.

The tests may also be given to the same children more than once. The minor physical ailments or emotional disturbances not uncommon amongst young children may influence individual scores on any given testing occasion. Children who might be so affected should have the opportunity on a subsequent occasion of showing what they really can do. For the reasons suggested, individual scores may sometimes show marked difference on the occasion of a second testing. If a whole group is tested a second time the second mean score may be expected to show a very slight increase over the first (in the region of 3 per cent—*i.e.*, 2 marks). This slight improvement may be attributed to increased familiarity with the group-test situation rather than to remembering the pattern of correct answers. (The reliability coefficient[1] for the battery is: $r = 0.84$.)

[1] See Chapter 7, pp. 87*n* and 88.

Conditions for Testing

The equipment used should be in good condition, free from wow and flutter and any other distortion. The loud-speaker should be so placed, and the volume so adjusted, that all the children can hear everything clearly without strain. All should sit facing the loud-speaker.

The test administrator should inform the children that they must listen carefully to the instructions, which tell them exactly what to do, and warn them not to shuffle, speak, or make any other sounds, as these would interfere with the listening of others as well as themselves. The following advice also proves cheerfully effective: "You should not look at your neighbour's answer; but if, by accident, your eye strays, and you see that your neighbour has written a different answer from yours, don't alter your own answer; and don't tell your neighbour—he is wrong!"

A copy of the answer form, the instructions and examples, and details of all the items of the battery follow.

TEXTS OF THE INSTRUCTIONS FOR THE TESTS

Pitch Discrimination Test

"Test number one—pitch. Listen to these two sounds" (item 2—semitone up); "the second sound is higher than the first and has moved 'up'. Listen to these two sounds" (item 1—semitone down); "now the second sound is lower than the first; it has moved 'down'. The next two sounds" (item 9—'same') "are the same. Some of the sounds you will hear are much closer together than you might expect. Listen to these" (item 12—6 c.p.s. difference up); "the second sound goes 'up'

MEASURES OF MUSICAL ABILITIES—Arnold Bentley

Name.. School..

Sex............... Age:.........years.........months. Class.............. Date...........................

I	II	III	IV
PITCH		CHORDS	

PITCH

I	
2	
3	
4	
5	
6	
7	
8	
9	
10	
11	
12	
13	
14	
15	
16	
17	
18	
19	
20	

TUNES

I	
2	
3	
4	
5	
6	
7	
8	
9	
10	

CHORDS

I	
2	
3	
4	
5	
6	
7	
8	
9	
10	
11	
12	
13	
14	
15	
16	
17	
18	
19	
20	

RHYTHM

I	
2	
3	
4	
5	
6	
7	
8	
9	
10	

Total
Score ....

from the first. Now listen to one that goes 'down' " (item 13—6 c.p.s. difference down). "So; if the second sound is the same as the first, write 'S'; if the second sound goes up, write 'U'; if the second sound goes down, write 'D'. Is that clear? 'S' for same; 'U' for up; 'D' for down. I shall call out each number as we come to it."

Tonal Memory Test

"Test number two—tunes. For each item two tunes will be played, like this" (second half of item 4, repeated). "If the second tune is the same as the first, as that was, write 'S'. If the second tune is not the same as the first, one note will have been changed. Listen to this example, and count the notes as they are played" (item 10). "In the second tune the third note is changed, and you would write the figure '3'. Listen to it again, and don't forget to count" (item 10). "So; if the third note is changed you will write the figure '3'; if the fourth note is changed you will write the figure '4'; if the second note is changed you will write the figure '2'; and so on. All the tunes have five notes; count them as they are played."

Chord Analysis Test

"Test number three—chords. You will hear chords; that means groups of notes played together. For example, here is a chord containing two notes. Listen to the two notes played separately" (example); "and again, together, as a chord" (chord repeated). "Here is another chord containing three notes. Listen to the three notes played separately" (example); "and together, as a chord" (chord repeated).

"Now listen to a chord containing four notes ; here are the four notes played separately" (example); "and together, as a chord" (chord repeated). "In the test the notes will not be played separately; they will be played together, as chords. Listen carefully, and write down the number of notes you hear in each chord."

Rhythmic Memory Test

"Test number four—rhythm. You will hear two patterns of notes. Each pattern has four beats, or pulses, like this:

One two three four ; or like this:

One two three four . If the second

pattern is the same as the first, write 'S', for 'same'; if the second pattern is different from the first, write down the number of the beat or pulse that is changed. Listen to this example, and see if you can decide which beat is changed:

One two three four

Yes, the third beat was changed. Here is another:

One two three four

There the second beat was changed. And another:

One two three four

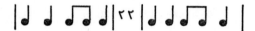

Those were the same. Your answer will be either 1 or 2 or 3 or 4 if there is a change, or S if the two patterns are the same. Now here is the test."

TABLE II. PITCH DISCRIMINATION TEST—PITCH
DIFFERENCES USED

Item	Direction of movement	Difference as fraction of a semitone	Difference in c.p.s.	First sound c.p.s.	Second sound c.p.s.
1	Down	1	26	440	414
2	Up	1	26	440	466
3	Up	$\frac{3}{4}$	18	440	458
4	Down	$\frac{3}{4}$	18	440	422
5	Up	$\frac{1}{2}$	12	440	452
6	Down	$\frac{1}{2}$	12	440	428
7	Down	c. 5/13	10	440	430
8	Up	c. 5/13	10	440	450
9	Same	—	—	440	440
10	Up	c. 4/13	8	440	448
11	Down	c. 4/13	8	440	432
12	Up	c. 3/13	6	440	446
13	Down	c. 3/13	6	440	434
14	Down	c. 5/26	5	440	435
15	Up	c. 5/26	5	440	445
16	Same	—	—	440	440
17	Up	c. 2/13	4	440	444
18	Down	c. 2/13	4	440	436
19	Down	c. 3/26	3	440	437
20	Up	c. 3/26	3	440	443

ITEMS OF THE TONAL MEMORY, RHYTHMIC MEMORY, AND CHORD ANALYSIS TESTS

Tonal Memory Test

Rhythmic Memory Test

Chord Analysis Test

7 The New Test Battery on Test

Validity—Reliability—Relationships between the individual tests of the battery—Influence of sex—Influence of intelligence

No test, no examination, no measurement of human abilities, is perfect. The most we can hope to achieve are the best tests that human fallibility, both on the part of the person making the tests and of those who are tested, will allow. We must accept this limitation. However, having done so, we must then submit the tests to the most rigorous scrutiny possible, to see if they measure up to certain minimum acceptable standards.

We ask such questions as: (1) Are they valid? *I.e.*, do they measure what they set out to measure? (2) Are they reliable? *I.e.*, are the results consistent if the tests are given to the same subjects on more than one occasion? A test which suggests that a child is a genius on one occasion and a moron on another occasion is obviously unreliable. (3) Do they overlap? *I.e.*, do the separate tests measure separate judgment functions? If, for instance, our pitch discrimination and tonal memory tests were found to be measuring the same judgment function, then no useful purpose would be served in spending time upon working both tests; a single test would suffice. (4) Are the tests influenced by sex? (5) Are they influenced by intelligence? We shall attempt to answer all these questions.

VALIDITY

Are the tests valid? Do they actually measure what they set out to measure—some aspects of musical ability? This is the most difficult question of all to answer because, as the reader is already aware from the discussion in Chapter 1, we cannot define musical ability except in the most general of terms. So we have to resort to such means as are available in deciding if the tests are valid. What are these means?

First of all we turn for help to those who are in constant close contact with many children, their class-teachers. Year after year they deal with large numbers of children, and come to know them well, their personalities, their likes and dislikes, and their varying abilities. Not all class-teachers are willing to give an opinion concerning a child's musical abilities; neither are all adequately equipped to do so. Moreover, class-teachers' assessments may be influenced by non-musical factors, such as co-operation or lack of it, which it is by no means easy to isolate in the making of subjective judgments. However, in the main, the judgments of class-teachers are useful as one means of deciding if a battery of tests is valid. At the very least if the designer of a test found that his results were in all respects diametrically opposite to the considered opinions of not one, but a large number of class-teachers, then he would be well advised to re-examine his basic assumptions, his test-structure, and the methods of application.

In order to compare the scores with class-teachers' assessments of musical ability, the test battery was given to 314 boys and girls; before the answer-papers were marked their class-teachers—forty-seven of them in thirty-five different schools—gave their own subjective assessments of the children's musical abilities on a four-point scale: A = musical; B = fairly musical; C = not very musical; D = unmusical. The test papers were then marked, and the pupils' scores compared with their class-teachers' assessments.

The statistical procedure that was used for the comparison is known as 'chi-squared'. This starts from the hypothesis that there is *no* association between the two variables under scrutiny—in this case the test scores on the one hand and the class-teachers' assessments on the other. In the present instance the chi-squared null-hypothesis was disproved at the 1 per cent significance level.[1] We may therefore assume that there *was* an association between the test scores and the teachers' assessments; and in general it was found that children who were assessed as 'musical' or 'fairly musical' scored the higher marks in the tests, just as those who scored the lower marks had been classified as 'unmusical' or 'not very musical'.

This method of assessing the validity of the tests may not be highly critical, but the results are not to be lightly dismissed; moreover, they may be checked against other additional criteria.

A further check on the validity of the new test battery was made with the help of a specialist string-class teacher, who

[1] This means that the probability of obtaining results as suggestive as the present results of a real association, when in fact there is no such association, is less than one in a hundred.

spent most of her time teaching individuals and small groups of children to play the violin and violoncello in several schools. Now, whereas the class-teachers had been asked to assess over a very wide ability range, from 'musical' to 'unmusical', the string-class teacher was dealing with a comparably smaller range of ability. Children who are sufficiently interested to want to try their hand at playing the violin are unlikely, at the very least, to be thoroughly 'unmusical'. We may assume, then, that the string-teacher's population sample contained a majority of children who were likely to be 'musical' or 'fairly musical'. Within this narrower range of ability her assessments had to be finer than those required of the class-teachers. However, she was better equipped to make such assessments, being trained as both musician and teacher, and she had a more specific criterion on which to base her assessments: progress in string-playing. She was asked to rate this progress on a four-point scale: A = good progress; B = fair progress; C = slow progress; D = little or no progress. These assessments were then compared with the scores achieved by her pupils in the test battery. Again the chi-squared statistical procedure was used. With a population sample of 116 children the null-hypothesis was again disproved, this time at the 2 per cent significance level. We may therefore assume that there was an association between the abilities measured by the tests and progress in string-playing.

The first progress reports had been given after a period of some three months' instruction. Further reports were obtained on sixty-five of the same children at the end of fifteen months' instruction. In the meantime there had been a change of string-teacher; but again there was a significant association between the test scores and the new teacher's assessment of progress.

The evidence so far obtained suggests that there may be some connection between musical ability and what the tests measure; but the reader who is unfamiliar with statistical procedures must be warned against jumping to the conclusion that anything in the nature of cause and effect is proved. We have not proved that the child who scores high marks in the tests will therefore make rapid progress in string-playing. We have not proved that the child who scores high marks is therefore 'musical'. What we have done is to produce evidence that there is a significant and positive degree of association between the test scores and the considered opinions of responsible teachers; this at least is encouraging.

Another way of checking the validity of the tests is to try them out on highly skilled musicians—*i.e.*, on those about whose outstanding ability in music there can be no doubt. If such subjects score badly in the tests, then it would be well to reconsider both the construction of the tests and the fundamental hypotheses. On the other hand, if they score well this may be regarded as evidence that (*a*) the quality of the recording and reproduction is adequate, and (*b*) the content of the tests is such as to arouse and sustain, for at least some twenty minutes, the interest of trained minds that think very largely in terms of musical sounds.

The test battery was submitted to this fairly stringent examination. Three distinct groups worked the tests:

    (1) 120 graduates in music—*i.e.*, those who held university degrees in music and/or graduate-equivalent diplomas from colleges of music. Ages ranged from 21 to 65 years.

(2) 22 professional string-teachers, none of whom was a music graduate, but 13 of whom held professional diplomas in music. Ages ranged from 20 to 66 years.

(3) 18 boy choral scholars of a university college chapel and school, selected for their scholarships on a combination of quality of voice, proved musical ability, and adequate general scholastic attainment for their age. Ages ranged from 7 years 7 months to 13 years 0 months, and the mean age of this group was 10 years 10 months.

In the following table we see the range of scores and the mean scores achieved by these three groups:

TABLE III. FULL TEST BATTERY—MEANS AND RANGES OF SCORES—MUSICALLY SELECTED GROUPS

| Group | Scores obtained (max: 60 = 100 per cent) | | | |
| | Range | | Mean | |
	Actual	As percentage	Actual	As percentage
120 graduates	60^1–47^2	100 per cent–78 per cent	55·5	92 per cent
22 string-teachers	58–43	97 per cent–72 per cent	52·0	87 per cent
18 choral scholars	57–38	95 per cent–63 per cent	48·8	81 per cent

[1] Of the 120 music graduates, only 4 obtained full marks—*i.e.*, 3 per cent of the total number taking the tests.
[2] Only one graduate scored less than 50 marks—*i.e.*, 83 per cent.

The highly skilled in music, both children and adults, scored well in the test battery. This, again, may not prove anything in the nature of cause and effect, but it suggests that there is a strong, positive association between what the tests measure and the functioning of acknowledged musical minds.

Our fourth means of assessing the validity of the tests is to compare the scores with the results of music examinations that are already established. Care has to be exercised here because the examinations used in the comparison must be concerned solely with musical skills; knowledge *about* music, such as dates, details of the lives of composers, the meanings of 'musical terms' like largo, allegro, pianissimo, and so on—in fact, anything that could be learnt by an intelligent but stone-deaf person—is irrelevant to our present purpose.

One type of examination that we were able to use as a further check on the validity of the test battery was that used for the selection of boys for choral scholarships in the university college chapel and choir school already mentioned. Periodically a small number of boys is selected from a much larger number of candidates. The Organist and Fellow of the College respons-ible for the music examines all the candidates in various aspects of music practice: vocal quality and range are of obvious im-portance, but much weight is also given to such abilities as memory for tunes played, interval and scale singing, rhythm tests, and, where applicable, instrumental performance—in fact, all aspects of music practice considered necessary and desirable in a good chorister. The selector is looking for general musical as well as specifically vocal abilities.

On four successive occasions the test battery was given to all the candidates for choral scholarships, but the scores were not disclosed until the final selection had been made by the normal musical methods. Then the results were compared. On the first occasion, out of a total of twenty-six candidates, three of the top four boys in the test-battery scores were selected. On the second occasion, out of a total of twenty-two candidates, four were selected from the first nine in order of scoring in the tests. On the third occasion, from fifteen candidates, the only choral scholar selected by the normal means was the boy who scored the highest marks in the tests. On the fourth occasion there were twenty-seven candidates; three of the top five boys in the tests were selected. On all occasions the boys who were quickly eliminated from the competition on the basis of the organist's entirely independent judgments were found to be those who had recorded the lower scores in the tests.

Thus we see that there was a high degree of correspondence between the scores obtained in the tests, which set out to measure some aspects of musical ability, and the assessments of musical ability made by a responsible, experienced, and highly qualified musician and teacher.

Another examination was also used as a check on validity, this time with seventy boys in their first year in a Grammar School. The examination took place at the end of twelve weeks' class work in music. The tests had been given at the beginning of the same term, when the mean age was 11 years 7 months, within a range of 11 years 1 month to 12 years 0 months. The examination consisted entirely of tests of musical skills taught during the term: singing a melody at sight from music notation, singing back a melody played to them, and writing from dictation melodic and rhythmic figures.

The distributions of the test-battery scores and the marks obtained twelve weeks later in the examination were almost identical, and both were near normal.[1]

[1] 'Normal' distribution of scores or marks implies that the bulk of the subjects score a mark close to the mean score of the group

Since the test scores and examination marks were normally distributed it was permissible to calculate a numerical figure known as the correlation coefficient.[1]

When the correlation coefficient for the test battery and the examination marks of these seventy boys was calculated it was found to be: r = 0·94. This indicates an extremely close correspondence between the two sets of figures.[2]

---

tested, and the rest distribute themselves, with decreasing frequency, symmetrically on either side of this mean. An approximation to such a distribution would look as follows:

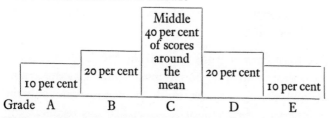

| Grade A | B | C | D | E |

We have quoted this particular distribution because this is the one that is used again in Chapter 8 (see p. 102 below). The reader who wishes to pursue this topic further should consult an elementary textbook of statistics.

[1] The correlation coefficient is normally referred to as 'r'. The figure calculated indicates the degree of correspondence between two normally distributed sets of figures. The positive range of 'r' is from o to 1; if o is the answer to the calculation there is no correlation whatever; the higher the correlation coefficient the greater is the degree of correspondence between the two sets of variables; but in the measurement of human abilities a complete correlation, signified by the answer 1, never occurs.

[2] So close was this indicated correspondence that a further check was made. All the subjects were arranged in order of placing by the test battery, from first to seventieth, and this rank order was compared with the rank order obtained in the end-of-term examination. The answer to this calculation is referred to as 'rho'; rho was calculated as 0·90, thus confirming the r = 0·94.

Again, then, we discover a high degree of correspondence between the scores obtained in the test battery and the marks obtained in an examination of musical skills conducted by an experienced music specialist teacher.

Such is the evidence concerning the validity of the tests. It is based upon four external criteria:

(1) class-teachers' estimates of musical ability;
(2) progress in a branch of musical activity;
(3) the performances in the tests of highly skilled musicians; and
(4) comparison with other established examination techniques.

We have been at pains to stress human fallibility and to warn against jumping to unwarranted conclusions concerning cause and effect. However, in all the comparisons with the four external criteria a positive association was revealed, and the indications are that the test battery accomplishes that for which it was devised—namely, the measurement of some aspects of musical ability.

RELIABILITY

We now turn to our second question: are the tests reliable? Do they produce consistent results when given to the same subjects on different occasions? The reliability of a test is easier to measure in numerical terms than its validity. The test may be given to the same subjects a second or third time, and the results of the different trials compared. If the subsequent results are consistent with the results of the first trial, then the test is reliable. If the subsequent results are wildly different from the first, then the test is unreliable, subject unduly to guessing and chance, and in general a waste of time.

In order to discover the reliability of the test battery it was given twice to ninety boys and girls whose ages ranged from 9 years 10 months to 11 years 9 months; the mean age was 10 years 9 months. The second trial took place four months after the first, and there was no chance of the children remembering their previous answers. The scores for each trial were normally distributed, so it was possible to calculate the correlation coefficient. This turned out to be: $r = 0.84$. Bearing in mind the age of the children, the fact that they were not a musically selected group, and the additional fact that the test battery is limited to sixty items, this figure of 0.84 may be regarded as satisfactory. We may reasonably conclude that the tests are reliable and not unduly subject to chance and guessing.

RELATIONSHIPS BETWEEN THE INDIVIDUAL TESTS OF THE BATTERY

The next question that we ask is: do the tests overlap? Do they measure separate judgment functions? Since they are all concerned with some aspect of musical ability it would not be surprising to find some degree of overlap; in fact, there is very little.

Two separate checks were made to discover the degree of relationship between the individual tests. In the first check the population sample was the same as that used for measuring reliability on re-test—*i.e.*, ninety boys and girls aged nine to eleven years. Correlation coefficients were calculated, and these may be seen in the first of the two tables. For the second check the population sample was 149 boys and girls, aged 11 years, and all of I.Q. 100 or above, and for this sample the chi-squared statistical procedure was used.

TABLE IV. RELATIONSHIPS BETWEEN THE INDIVIDUAL
TESTS—CORRELATION COEFFICIENTS

Test	Tonal memory	Chord analysis	Rhythmic memory
Pitch discrimination	0·47	0·40	0·25
Tonal memory	—	0·41	0·34
Chord analysis	—	—	0·40

Notes. (1) Pitch discrimination/rhythmic memory just significant @ 5 per cent level.
(2) All the rest significant @ 1 per cent level.

TABLE V. RELATIONSHIPS BETWEEN THE INDIVIDUAL
TESTS—RESULTS OF CHI-SQUARED CALCULATIONS

Test	Tonal memory	Chord analysis	Rhythmic memory
Pitch discrimination	Sig. @ 1 per cent	Sig. @ 1 per cent	Not sig.
Tonal memory	—	Sig. @ 5 per cent	Not. sig.
Chord analysis	—	—	Not. sig.

Note. Sig. = significant

Three of the higher figures of Table IV (for pitch discrimination/tonal memory, pitch discrimination/chord analysis, and tonal memory/chord analysis) correspond with the significant associations of Table V; whereas the two lowest figures of Table IV (for pitch discrimination/rhythmic memory and tonal memory/rhythmic memory) correspond with 'not significant' results of Table V. The figure of 0·40 for chord analysis/rhythmic memory in Table IV was a surprise, but it is not supported by a significant association in Table V; the latter corresponds more nearly with the expectations of the musician in so far as it shows no significant association between rhythmic memory and the other three tests.

All the correlation coefficients in Table IV are small, and would indicate only a very low forecasting efficiency. According to Sumner (1948, p. 48), "the forecasting efficiency of 'r' = 0·4 is 8·4 per cent, i.e. prediction is only 8·4 per cent better than pure chance."

Had any of the correlation coefficients in Table IV been high, and at the same time been confirmed by significant associations in Table V, suspicion would have been aroused that the two tests of any pair involved might have been measuring the same kind of judgment function.

Perhaps the most interesting relationship is that for tonal memory/rhythmic memory; a low correlation coefficient (0·34) in Table IV and a 'not significant' association in Table V. Teachers know that the tonal and rhythmic aspects of memory are sometimes profitably distinguished in the learning process. The data obtained from the earlier pilot test of memory had led to the decision to measure these two aspects separately; confidence in that decision is increased by the present findings of a low correlation on the one hand and the 'not significant' association on the other.

All the different functions measured by the four tests operate, in varying degrees and both separately and together, in music-making. Practical experience suggests that, although they usually seem to be working all together, they are in fact separable functions. The results here given may be regarded as justification of the attempt to measure them separately.

INFLUENCE OF SEX

Out next question concerns sex and musical abilities. Is there any difference between the scores of boys and those of girls? The short answer is no. The scores of 590 boys and 566 girls between the ages of eight and twelve years were compared. The mean score for the boys was 30·1, that for the girls 30·9. The difference in favour of the girls was 0·8 out of a possible 60—*i.e.*, 1·25 per cent.

In another calculation on 118 boys and 152 girls, all aged 11 years, it was found that such differences as there were between the mean scores of boys and girls were not significant, either for the full test battery or for any of the individual tests.

INFLUENCE OF INTELLIGENCE

Are the test scores influenced by the intelligence of the subject? Do the tests measure not only some aspects of musical ability but also intelligence? If intelligence unduly influences the scores, then the tests are not measuring musical abilities as distinct from intelligence. Of course, it might be maintained that it is not possible to make this distinction, on the grounds that the expert adult musician must be intelligent; otherwise he would not have achieved his musical eminence. On the other hand, many other adults of extremely high intelligence evince little interest or ability in music.

Similarly with young children. Their intelligence, or some aspects of intelligence, can be measured objectively and the results expressed as an Intelligence Quotient (I.Q.). If we accept I.Q.s as valid measures of intelligence we can then usefully compare them with musical-ability test scores. When the distributions of both I.Q.s and the test scores are normal we can calculate a correlation coefficient, as was done when we examined the reliability of the tests. If the correlation coefficient is high—*i.e.*, approaching 1—then there is a high correspondence between intelligence and those aspects of musical ability measured by the tests; the judgment functions required by either test are similar, and there is no point in using separate tests merely to measure more or less the same thing. However, if the discovered correlation coefficient is low, then separate tests are necessary to measure the separate abilities involved.

A group of 166 children was selected on the basis of an I.Q. distribution approximating to the normal curve.[1] The range of I.Q.s was from 70 to 140+; the mean I.Q. was 101; and the standard deviation was 11·0. The test scores of these children were correlated with their I.Q.s, and the correlation coefficients are shown in Table VI:

TABLE VI. RELATIONSHIPS BETWEEN I.Q. AND THE INDIVIDUAL TESTS

I.Q. and pitch discrimination:	$r = 0.30$
I.Q. and tonal memory:	$r = 0.25$
I.Q. and chord analysis:	$r = 0.24$
I.Q. and rhythmic memory:	$r = 0.34$
I.Q. and full test battery:	$r = 0.38$
All significant @ 1 per cent level	

[1] All the I.Q.s had been measured by one test—the Moray House Verbal Reasoning Test.

M.A.C.—G

The reader will observe that all the correlation coefficients are low. If, on the basis of these figures, I.Q.s were used to predict musical abilities the forecasting efficiency would be even smaller than that mentioned on page 91 above. Other investigators in this field have also found that the relationship between musical ability, as measured by various tests, and intelligence, also measured by various tests, commonly reveals a positive correlation where 'r' is used; but, as in the present case, the correlation is usually low.

In another check on 149 boys and girls, all aged 11 years and all of I.Q. = 100 or above, it was found by using chi-squared that there was no significant association between I.Q. and tonal memory, I.Q. and rhythmic memory, and I.Q. and chord analysis; the only significant association discovered was between I.Q. and pitch discrimination.

Thus we have evidence from the use of two different statistical procedures on two different but comparably similar population samples. The first revealed a positive, significant, but only small degree of correlation between all the tests and I.Q.; the other revealed a significant association only between pitch discrimination and I.Q., and none between I.Q. and the other three tests.

Examination of individual scores further reveals that many subjects of relatively low I.Q. scored high music-test marks, and that others of high I.Q. scored low music-test marks. A few examples of this are given below, where grade A represents the top 10 per cent of the scores in the music tests, grade B the next 20 per cent, grade C the middle 40 per cent, grade D the next lower 20 per cent, and grade E the lowest 10 per cent.

Grade in the music tests	I.Q.s of some of the subjects
A	101, 104, 106, 108
B	89, 91, 101
C	84, 87, 89, 90
D	112, 117, 121, 139
E	101, 123

It could be maintained that a certain degree of intelligence is required in order to understand and carry out the instructions of the present or any other group-tests. It was in order to reduce to a minimum any such demand upon intelligence, as distinct from the musical abilities we were seeking to measure, that so much care was taken over the instructions of the present tests. It will be recalled that they were tried out, modified, and simplified until they were proved to be intelligible on a single hearing and without interpretation to the majority of the very youngest children likely to be subjected to the tests.

It may also be maintained that intelligence is likely to influence the performance of any task an individual undertakes, the degree of influence varying with the kind of task; and that it will also operate in any situation requiring judgments upon material presented to the subject, as in these tests and as in any music-making situation. However, it is important to emphasize the low correlations and 'not significant' associations discovered in dealing with young children, especially in view of the opinions of some instrumental teachers who maintain that I.Q. alone is a sufficient guide in the selection of children for instrumental tuition. Reservations concerning such dependence upon the forecasting efficiency of I.Q. for music-making are even more important when it is appreciated that I.Q. is commonly measured by tests of verbal reasoning; and the connection between verbal reasoning and the kind of judgments required in music practice is, at the least, not immediately apparent.

The available evidence, then, suggests that the influence of intelligence upon performance in these tests of musical abilities is either not significant or, at the most, very slight.

In this chapter we have, as it were, put the tests themselves on test. We first acknowledged their inevitable imperfections as measures of human abilities; we then posed a number of questions and answered them. No extravagant claims are made; nothing is final or conclusive; improvement may always be sought. But as far as we can ascertain from the evidence available, the tests are valid and reliable, they each measure a separate judgment function, they are not influenced by sex, and they are influenced only slightly by intelligence.

8 Musical Abilities and Chronological Age

Test battery scores in relation to chronological age—Disclosure of wide range of musical abilities at any given age—Musical Ability Age—Musical abilities appear to be largely innate—Grading of scores—Interpretation of the grades

TEST BATTERY SCORES IN RELATION TO CHRONO-LOGICAL AGE

Evidence has already been produced concerning the validity and reliability of the tests; it has also been seen that the functions of the separate tests do not overlap, that boys and girls score equally, and that intelligence has little influence on the scores. We shall now consider the test results in relation to chronological age.

At the time of writing the tests of the new battery have been used with some 2000 boys and girls between the ages of seven and fourteen years in normal school classes. The mean scores and ranges of scores (highest to lowest) for each age group, together with the yearly percentage increases, are given in Table VII. For purposes of comparison we also give the corresponding figures for the 18 choral scholars and the 120 music graduates already discussed in Chapter 7 (pp. 83–84), and for 350 musically unselected adult students in teacher training colleges.

TABLE VII. FULL TEST BATTERY—MEANS AND RANGES
OF SCORES FOR EACH AGE GROUP

Full test battery			
Age or group	Mean score	Range of scores	Yearly increase—per cent
7 years	20·4	43– 7	—
8 ,,	23·4	42– 7	5·0 per cent
9 ,,	25·6	48– 7	3·7 per cent
10 ,,	28·6	53–12	5·0 per cent
11 ,,	32·3	54–12	6·2 per cent
12 ,,	36·0	55–14	6·2 per cent
13 ,,	38·8	56–14	4·7 per cent
14 ,,	42·0	58–19	5·3 per cent
Choral scholars	48·8	57–38	—
Music graduates	55·5	60–47	—
Other adults —unselected	44·1	58–26	—

DISCLOSURE OF WIDE RANGE OF MUSICAL ABILITIES
AT ANY GIVEN AGE

We observe a small and steady yearly increase in the mean scores from the age of seven to that of fourteen years. The average yearly increase is 3 marks out of a possible 60—*i.e.*, 5 per cent. This is very small. It is the more noticeably so when compared with the wide range of scores recorded at any given chronological age. The smallest range of scores is 35 at the age of eight years (*i.e.*, 58 per cent); the biggest range is 42 at eleven and thirteen years (*i.e.*, 70 per cent); and the mean range of scores for the ages seven to fourteen years is 40 (*i.e.*, 67 per cent).

The scores of individual children, in comparison with the mean scores of their age group, are of special interest. Three seven-year-old children scored at least 36 (*i.e.*, the mean score of the twelve-year-old group), and one of these seven-year-olds scored 43. One twelve-year-old child scored 55 (*i.e.*, the mean score of the adult music graduates); one aged eleven years and one aged ten years scored 54 and 53 respectively. There are many other examples of individuals scoring much higher than the mean scores not only of their own age groups, but also of groups several years older, just as, of course, there are those scoring well below their chronological age means. Furthermore, these scores were recorded by very ordinary children, of wide general ability range, in ordinary State primary and secondary school classes. They were not specially selected, nor had they received any special musical training.

MUSICAL ABILITY AGE

This very wide range of musical abilities, as measured by the tests, is even more vividly revealed if we allow ourselves to speculate in terms of a Musical Ability Age. Now it so happens that if we divide the mean score for any age group by three the nearest whole-number answer is the age, in years, of that group. For instance, the mean score for the seven-year-olds is

20·4; this number divided by three yields the answer 6·8—
i.e., 7 nearest whole number. The mean score of the nine-year-
olds is 25·6; this divided by three yields 8·53—*i.e.*, 9 nearest
whole number. This difference of 0·47 from the whole number
is quoted as it is the biggest of all such differences. All the rest
are smaller deviations from their nearest whole numbers, and
some mean scores divide exactly into the mean ages of the
group—*e.g.*, at twelve and fourteen years. In other words, the
mean Musical Ability Age of any group is the same as the
chronological age of that group.

Applying the simple formula $\dfrac{\text{Score}}{3}$, we find in any chronological age group Musical Ability Ages ranging over some
thirteen to fourteen years. For instance, at the chronological
age of ten years scores range from 12 to 53—*i.e.*, Musical
Ability Ages range from four to eighteen years. Now our actual
figures do not account for children under the age of seven
years, nor over the age of fourteen years. But, even discounting
speculation outside these ages, and concentrating on the
actual figures available, at any chronological age between seven
and fourteen years we find a Musical Ability Age range of at
least seven years. Some seven-year-olds score above the mean
of the fourteen-year-olds, and some fourteen-year-olds score
below the mean of the seven-year-olds.

MUSICAL ABILITIES APPEAR TO BE LARGELY INNATE

A wide range of musical abilities as measured by their tests
has also been demonstrated by Wing (1948) and Kwalwasser
(1955), who in the main were dealing with older children. We
now have evidence from tests especially devised for younger

children that similar wide ranges of abilities already exist in children as young as seven years of age. Kwalwasser (1955) states:

> music is both a non-factual subject and one remotely related to intelligence and chronological age. . . . In every so called grade [*i.e.*, school class or year grouping] there are multiple grades in music. In the fifth grade, for example, you will find superior music talents comparable to those in conservatories and colleges, and you will also find music talents so poor that the kindergarten classification would be most flattering.

Kwalwasser inclined to the inherited-talent school of thought discussed in Chapter 1. When it is remembered that the children tested in the present investigation came from not very dissimilar social and domestic environments, and had had similar training in schools, one cannot avoid the conclusion that the abilities disclosed are to a great extent innate.[1]

GRADING OF SCORES

In Chapter 1 it was stated that measurement implies comparison and involves numerical quantities. This, of course, is the object of measurement, and the making of distinctions and borderlines is inherent in it. The present tests are an attempt to make such measurements, comparisons, and distinctions. However, as they do not profess to be more than a general guide,

---

[1] Some support for this conclusion comes from the recent researches of Shuter (1964), who compared the Wing test scores of identical with fraternal twins, and of children and their parents. The main conclusion she drew from her review of past research and her own investigation was that "there is an important genetic component in musical ability which may set an upper limit to achievement and speed of learning." (Shuter, 1964, p. 411.)

only five musical ability grades were calculated for each chronological age group. Scores for each grade are shown in Table VIII below. Grade A represents the top 10 per cent of the population of an age group, Grade B the next lower 20 per cent, Grade C the middle 40 per cent, Grade D the next lower 20 per cent, and Grade E the lowest 10 per cent. Finer distinctions would be neither justified nor necessary for practical purposes.

TABLE VIII. GRADING OF SCORES

Age in years	Grade A top 10 per cent	Grade B 20 per cent	Grade C middle 40 per cent	Grade D 20 per cent	Grade E bottom 10 per cent
	at least				at most
7	33	32–23	22–17	16–14	13
8	36	35–27	26–20	19–14	13
9	39	38–31	30–21	20–15	14
10	41	40–34	33–23	22–18	17
11	44	43–38	37–29	28–22	21
12	47	46–42	41–31	30–23	22
13	48	47–44	43–35	34–25	24
14	51	50–46	45–39	38–31	30

Remembering that we are dealing with dynamic human material that refuses to be absolutely constant from day to day, we must interpret these grades, and particularly the border-line cases, intelligently. For example, at the chronological age of nine years the score of 38 falls into Grade B, but it is almost in Grade A; whereas a score of 34 is comfortably in the middle of Grade B, and a score of 31, whilst also in Grade B, is almost in Grade C. If a decision must be reached concerning selection or rejection of children with border-line scores, the best solution is to repeat the tests and also take into account other factors such as determination, likely domestic encouragement for practice, conflicting interests, and so on.

INTERPRETATION OF THE GRADES

In interpreting the test scores and grades it may be safely assumed that children classified in Grade A are the most likely to succeed in musical activities requiring superior abilities; then those in Grade B. These two grades comprise 30 per cent of the population, which is probably considerably in excess of the proportion of the population as a whole taking an active part in practical music-making in anything more than the most casual way. It does not follow that some children in the lower grades, according to their test scores, would not gain something from extra musical activities, nor that they should be denied the opportunity to take part in them, if room can be found and the facilities are available. Such decisions are best made by the teacher on the spot, who knows all the circumstances. But where facilities are limited, as they usually are, and it is imperative that optimum use be made of both time and material, then the test scores and grades can be a useful guide to the selection of those who are likely to gain most from the facilities available.

Furthermore, in music it is especially important to discover outstanding abilities, and to encourage the practical application of them, at an early age. On the other hand, it is no kindness to a child to encourage him to try to achieve special skills for which he does not possess the inherent abilities and when his only reward is likely to be lack of achievement and its consequent frustration, disappointment, and loss of self-esteem.

The question may be asked: how reliable are the grades? Is it likely that a child would be graded as C on one occasion of testing and as A or E on another? The statistical reliability of the test battery is 0·84 (see Chapter 7, p. 89). A further check was made on the reliability of the grading, using eighty-five boys and girls who worked the tests twice, once at the age of ten years and the second time a year later. Table IX gives the results of this check:

TABLE IX. MOVEMENT BETWEEN GRADES ON SUBSEQUENT TESTING

Remaining in same grade	Moving to an adjacent grade		Moving two grades	
	Upwards	Downward	Upward	Downward
36 = 42·4 per cent	23 = 27·1 per cent	20 = 23·5 per cent	3 = 3·5 per cent	3 = 3·5 per cent
36 = 42·4 per cent	43 = 50·6 per cent		6 = 7·0 per cent	

Note. There was a full range of grades from A to E.

Examination of the table reveals that 42 per cent remained in the same grade from one year to the next; that 51 per cent moved one grade, with almost equal numbers moving up and down; and that only 7 per cent moved two grades. No child moved more than two grades.

The smallest difference in score needed for re-grading— for instance, from C to A or vice versa—at ten years of age is 8 marks; at eleven years of age it is 7 marks. A difference of a single mark on the borderline can result in a different grading. This is a normal eventuality in the making of any form of measurement and distinctions, and in this check on the reliability of the grading a number of border-line and near-border-line cases were involved. The results, then, are by no means unsatisfactory. The fact that only 7 per cent moved two grades after the interval of a year, and that none moved more than two grades, inspires confidence both in the tests and in the grading; but, as has already been stressed, the grades must be interpreted intelligently and not regarded as final, irrevocable "revelations of destiny".

9 *What do we learn from the Individual Tests?*

*Relative difficulty of the tests—Pitch discrimination—
Memory: Tonal memory—Rhythmic memory—Chord analysis—
Summary of findings*

We have already discussed the full battery scores in relation to
chronological age. We now turn to examine in greater detail
the results obtained from the individual tests.

RELATIVE DIFFICULTY OF THE TESTS

In the first place we consider the relative difficulty of the tests
for the whole age range of children tested—*i.e.*, seven to
fourteen years—and for the 18 choral scholars, 120 music
graduates, and 350 musically unselected adults. The mean
scores of these groups are given in Table X.

We observe that the rhythmic memory test proved easier
than the tonal memory test, and that each of these was easier
than either of the other two tests; chord analysis proved the
most difficult for all except the music graduates. We do not
attach any significance to the fact that this expert group of

adults scored marginally higher in chord analysis than in pitch discrimination. The tests were devised for young children, and not in order to distinguish fine differences amongst those who are already acknowledged experts.

It is interesting to note that the choral scholars, whose mean age was 10 years 10 months within a range of 7 years 7 months to 13 years 0 months, achieved much higher mean scores than the group of musically unselected adults, especially in pitch discrimination and chord analysis. We may also note that the choral scholars achieved higher scores in tonal memory than in rhythmic memory—*i.e.*, the opposite of the results obtained from the musically unselected children of seven to fourteen years.

TABLE X. FULL TEST BATTERY—MEAN SCORES

Mean scores expressed as percentages				
Group	Pitch discrimination	Tonal memory	Rhythmic memory	Chord analysis
Children aged 7 to 14 years	53 per cent	56 per cent	64 per cent	37 per cent
		combined 60 per cent		
Choral scholars	80 per cent	93 per cent	83 per cent	76 per cent
		combined 88 per cent		
Music graduates	88 per cent	98 per cent	95 per cent	92 per cent
		combined 96·5 per cent		
Other adults— unselected	71 per cent	86 per cent	86 per cent	62 per cent
		combined 86 per cent		

Having compared the four tests, we will now examine the results of each separate test in greater detail.

PITCH DISCRIMINATION

As with the full battery, we find here a small and steady increase in mean scores with increasing age throughout childhood.

TABLE XI. PITCH DISCRIMINATION—MEANS AND RANGES OF SCORES FOR EACH AGE GROUP

Age or group	Mean score	Range of scores	Yearly increase —percentage
7 years	8·0	14–1	—
8 ,,	8·8	15–0	4·0 per cent
9 ,,	9·7	17–3	4·5 per cent
10 ,,	10·4	17–3	3·5 per cent
11 ,,	11·1	19–1	3·5 per cent
12 ,,	12·3	18–2	6·0 per cent
13 ,,	12·7	20–3	2·0 per cent
14 ,,	13·5	20–7	4·0 per cent
Choral scholars	16·1	19–12	—
Music graduates	17·7	20–13	—
Other adults —unselected	14·3	19–7	—

The table shows that not only do the mean scores increase steadily with age, but the highest scores achieved at each age also show an increase, although less steady from year to year. We observe that the mean score of the unselected adults was only 0·8 above the mean of the fourteen-year-olds—*i.e.*, an increase of only 4 per cent in a period of about six years. On the other hand, the mean score of the choral scholars was 1·8 (*i.e.*, 9 per cent) higher than that of the unselected adults, and 2·6 (*i.e.*, 13 per cent) above that of the fourteen-year-olds. We also observe that the range of scores at each age is many times greater than the mean increase from year to year. Whereas the mean yearly increase is in the region of 5 per cent, the mean range of scores for ages seven to fourteen years is 15 (*i.e.*, 75 per cent).

So far we have considered only mean scores and score ranges. What can we learn about the varying sizes of pitch difference in relation to age?

TABLE XII. PITCH DISCRIMINATION—MEAN ERRORS FOR DIFFERENT LEVELS OF PITCH DIFFERENCES

Mean errors expressed as percentages to nearest 5 per cent				
Age of group	Pitch differences in cycles per second			
	26	12	6	3
7 years	25	35	65	85
8 „	20	30	65	85
9 „	15	30	65	85
10 „	15	30	50	80
11 „	10	20	50	80
12 „	5	10	40	80
13 „	5	5	40	80
14 „	0	5	35	75
Choral scholars	0	0	10	40
Music graduates	0	0	0	15
Other adults—unselected	5	10	25	65

All the figures quoted in the table have been adjusted to the nearest 5 per cent. The degree of accuracy that might be implied by quoting such figures as 29 per cent or 31 per cent is not claimed. In any case, the strict absolute values of the figures are less important than the trends they reveal; and the trends become all the clearer when the figures are rounded up to the nearest 5 per cent. Again, in order to reveal the trends in the clearest possible way, we have quoted the errors for only four steps in the descending order of pitch differences, each column representing a pitch difference half the size of the one preceding: 26 c.p.s. (semitone), 12 c.p.s. (quarter-tone), 6 c.p.s. (eighth-tone), and 3 c.p.s. (approximately sixteenth-tone).

As the size of each pitch difference is halved, we see a large increase in the number of errors recorded in the majority of cases; the overall trend is for the number of errors to double as the size of the pitch difference is halved. We also note an improvement from seven to fourteen years, in the region of 30 per cent for the 26, 12, and 6 c.p.s. differences, but only 10 per cent at the 3 c.p.s. difference level. This last figure appears to confirm the decision reached earlier (Chapter 6, p. 60) that 3 c.p.s. is about the smallest pitch difference that may be usefully employed in a group-test reproduced by a loudspeaker with musically unselected children.

Reading down the columns we observe a gradual reduction in the number of errors as age increases; this would suggest that, between the ages of seven and fourteen years, ability to discriminate fine differences in pitch improves.

The table also shows that the majority of all the subjects, including the seven-year-olds, could discriminate quarter-tones (*i.e.*, 12 c.p.s. pitch differences) correctly, that about half the ten- and eleven-year-olds and the majority of the twelve-year-olds and older could judge eighth-tones accurately. The majority of the choral scholars and the music graduates judged all the pitch differences accurately, but errors at all the pitch difference levels were recorded by the musically unselected adults, and the majority of these failed to discriminate accurately differences of a sixteenth-tone (*i.e.*, 3 c.p.s.).

MEMORY

We have already seen that both the tonal and rhythmic memory tests were easier than the tests of pitch discrimination and chord analysis, and that the musically unselected children of seven to fourteen years found the rhythmic memory test easier than the tonal memory test. This may be taken to indicate that memory for rhythmic patterns is likely to develop earlier than any other aspect of musical ability. Observation of young children at play reveals that children tend to 'coalesce' with a dominant rhythmic pattern earlier and with greater spontaneity than they 'coincide' with a pitch pattern. (See Chapter 2.)

TONAL MEMORY

As in pitch discrimination, we again find a small and steady increase in mean scores with increasing age.

With the single exception of the seven-year-olds, in all age groups there were children who could score full marks; and in all age groups below fourteen years there were some who scored no marks. Up to the age of fourteen years the range of scores is virtually 100 per cent; in contrast with this, we find

TABLE XIII. TONAL MEMORY—MEANS AND RANGES OF
SCORES FOR EACH AGE GROUP

Age or group	Mean score	Range of scores	Yearly increase —percentage
7 years	2·6	9–0	—
8 ,,	3·9	10–0	13 per cent
9 ,,	4·7	10–0	8 per cent
10 ,,	5·6	10–0	9 per cent
11 ,,	6·4	10–0	8 per cent
12 ,,	6·9	10–0	5 per cent
13 ,,	7·5	10–0	6 per cent
14 ,,	8·2	10–3	7 per cent
Choral scholars	9·3	10–8	—
Music graduates	9·8	10–8	—
Other adults— unselected	8·6	10–2	—

that the mean yearly increase is in the region of 8 per cent.
Unselected adults score only 0·4 (*i.e.*, 4 per cent) better than
the fourteen-year-olds, whereas the choral scholars produce a
mean score of 1·1 (*i.e.*, 11 per cent) higher than the fourteen-
year-olds, and 0·7 (*i.e.*, 7 per cent) better than the unselected
adults.

Analysis of errors indicates that the two factors that affect
the degree of difficulty in remembering a purely tonal configuration are the serial position of a note in the tune and the
size of pitch interval involved. We shall deal with the serial
position first.

The reader will recall that the tonal memory test requires
subjects to remember in detail a tune of five pitch sounds, and
then to compare another tune of five sounds in which four

sounds are the same as in the first tune, but one note has been changed. The change must be located as: first, second, third, fourth, or fifth note.

The mean errors for the five serial position changes were as follows:

TABLE XIV. TONAL MEMORY—MEAN ERRORS FOR
DIFFERENT SERIAL POSITIONS OF CHANGED NOTE

Serial position of changed note	Mean errors as percentage
1	41·6 per cent
2	30·6 per cent
3	38·3 per cent
4	33·4 per cent
5	19·5 per cent

The last note was clearly the one most easily remembered, and the first was the most difficult to recall. There is not much difference in difficulty between the first and the third, nor again between the second and the fourth. In fact, apart from the last note, there is insufficient evidence for conclusions concerning the relative difficulty of the first four sounds.

The serial position factor in tonal memory merits further investigation. Ortmann (1926, p. 4) maintains that the first and last notes of a melody "are projected more vividly upon consciousness" than intermediate notes; and Francès (1954) found that the first and last notes were easier to remember than intermediate notes, but he treats the first and last notes together as a group, making no distinction between them. If we compare the mean errors for first-fifth (30·5 per cent) and second-third-fourth (34·1 per cent) we observe that the intermediate notes, as a group, are more difficult than the first and last, as a group; but the difference is small, and when we consider separately the errors on the first (41·6 per cent) and those on the fifth (19·5 per cent) we discover that the first was twice as difficult to remember as the fifth, and realize that such grouping as that used by Ortmann and Francès may give rise to misleading conclusions.

The other factor affecting the degree of difficulty in remembering a tonal configuration is the size of pitch interval involved. Semitone changes produced a mean error of 28·8 per cent, and were thus easier to judge correctly than changes of a whole-tone, whose mean error was 36·6 per cent. In other words, when attention was concentrated entirely on the tonal aspect of melody, chromatic changes of a semitone were more prominent than changes of a whole-tone within the established diatonic framework of the key.

The discovery that semitone changes were easier to detect than whole-tone changes appears to contradict the findings in the pilot test of memory. There the mean error for semitone changes (52 per cent) was larger than that for whole-tone changes (34 per cent), suggesting that semitones were more difficult to detect than whole-tones. (See Chapter 5, p. 47.) In the pilot memory test confusion arose from the interaction of as many as four factors in all the items; this has already been discussed; it was one of the reasons for subsequently making two separate tests of the tonal and rhythmic aspects of memory.

Although both the pilot test and the later tonal memory test are measures of memory, they are different in construction and detail. In the pilot test the tonal and rhythmic elements were combined; the tonal centre was moved from time to time; the lengths of the items ranged from three to ten notes; the note-lengths were not all equal; the pulse-groupings varied between the items: some were in three-pulse measure, some in four-pulse, and some in two-pulse compound time. In the later tonal memory test, which concentrates entirely on tonal configuration, the tonal centre is constant (Key D major) and all the notes lie within the fifth: d to a; all the items are of the same length (five notes); all the note-lengths are equal; all the notes are equally loud; and the rhythmic element is removed in so far as there are no intentional accents or pulse-groupings or subdivisions of pulse.

The findings of each test, although apparently contradictory, are substantiated by the respective scores and analyses of errors. This is an apt illustration of the difficulties involved in this kind of work, and of the danger of making generalizations from a single test. Each of the tests measures some aspects of memory for musical configurations—*i.e.*, those aspects that it sets out to measure or that it appears to measure—but caution is needed in interpreting the results. The control of all the different factors involved, by the elimination of each singly or otherwise, is not available in experiments involving judgments by young children to the same extent as is possible in a laboratory. For instance, one can never be sure of complete attention for the whole time, with the result that errors may not always be due so much to lack of ability to judge correctly as to temporary lapse of attention to detail.

However, two of at least four factors that had caused confusion in the pilot memory test were eliminated in the construction of the later tonal memory test; and since the latter now concentrates wholly on the tonal aspect of memory, we may have greater confidence in the results obtained from its use. We shall accept that, in a tonal configuration, a change of a chromatic semitone is more prominent than one of a whole-tone within the diatonic framework of the key.

RHYTHMIC MEMORY

Like the other tests, the rhythmic memory test reveals a fairly steady increase in mean scores from year to year.

TABLE XV. RHYTHMIC MEMORY—MEANS AND RANGES OF SCORES FOR EACH AGE GROUP

Age or group	Mean score	Range of scores	Yearly increase —percentage
7 years	3·9	9–0	—
8 ,,	5·5	10–0	16 per cent
9 ,,	5·7	10–1	2 per cent
10 ,,	6·4	10–1	7 per cent
11 ,,	6·9	10–0	5 per cent
12 ,,	7·3	10–1	4 per cent
13 ,,	8·0	10–1	7 per cent
14 ,,	8·8	10–5	8 per cent
Choral scholars	8·3	10–5	—
Music graduates	9·5	10–7	—
Other adults— unselected	8·6	10–4	—

With the single exception of the seven-year-olds, there were children in all age groups who scored full marks; and below the age of fourteen years there were always some who scored only one mark or none at all. Up to fourteen years the range of scores at all ages is between 90 per cent and 100 per cent, yet the mean yearly increase is only 7 per cent. We may observe that this was the only test in which the young choral scholars did not surpass the unselected adults and the fourteen-year-olds; and it is also the only test in which the mean score of the unselected adults is not higher than that of the fourteen-year-olds.

Mean scores for the serial position changes are:

Change on:	Mean score
1st pulse	72·3 per cent
3rd ,,	65·6 per cent
2nd ,,	61·8 per cent
4th ,,	58·7 per cent

This order corresponds with the normal subjectively assessed order of strength of pulse in quadruple time: first, third, second, fourth. However, no special significance is attached to this correspondence in view of the wide differences in errors recorded on some of the same-pulse change items. In addition to the serial position of the change, the kind of rhythmic figure involved in the change affects the difficulty or otherwise of remembering.

CHORD ANALYSIS

We have seen that this was the most difficult of the four tests in the battery for all groups except the music graduates, who scored a marginally higher mean in this test (92 per cent) than in the pitch discrimination test (88 per cent). The musically unselected children of seven to fourteen years found it much more difficult than the other tests.

Again we see that the mean scores increase steadily with increase in age, but the yearly increases between seven and ten years are very small, the bigger increases coming later. For the whole seven to fourteen age range the mean increase is in the region of 5 per cent per annum, but at all ages there is an extremely wide range of scores, averaging 80 per cent. It is not until the age of eleven years is reached that the mean score clearly exceeds the theoretical guessing score for the test (*i.e.*, 6·7). The choral scholars achieve a mean score of 3·7 (18·5 per cent) higher than the fourteen-year-olds, and 2·7 (13·5 per cent) higher than the unselected adults. The latter show an increase of only 1·0 (5 per cent) over the fourteen-year-olds.

TABLE XVI. CHORD ANALYSIS—MEANS AND RANGES OF SCORES FOR EACH AGE GROUP

Age or group	Mean score	Range of scores	Yearly increase —percentage
7 years	4·8	14–0	—
8 ,,	5·1	15–0	1·5 per cent
9 ,,	5·5	16–0	2·0 per cent
10 ,,	6·2	16–0	3·5 per cent
11 ,,	7·9	18–0	8·5 per cent
12 ,,	9·4	18–0	7·5 per cent
13 ,,	10·4	19–0	5·0 per cent
14 ,,	11·5	20–5	5·5 per cent
Choral scholars	15·2	20–11	—
Music graduates	18·4	20–14	—
Other adults— unselected	12·5	20–2	—

The very low mean scores of the younger age groups prompt us to ask if this test is unsuitable or too difficult for use as a group test with these younger children. If we consider only the mean scores the answer must be in the affirmative. However, as in the battery as a whole, we find that quite a number of these younger children score high marks. Taking as an arbitrary line of demarcation the score of 11 (*i.e.*, above half marks, and well above the theoretical guessing score), we discover that at least 14 per cent of ten-year-olds score 11 or more, 11 per cent of nine-year-olds, 7 per cent of eight-year-olds, and 11 per cent of seven-year-olds. The absolute values of these figures are of less importance than the firm indication that there are some young children, a by no means negligible proportion, who can make these judgments of chord analysis with much greater accuracy than the majority of their age group. Thus we may consider that this test, although difficult, is not unsuitable for use with younger children.

However, we may conclude that ability to analyse chords develops more slowly than the other aspects of musical ability measured by the battery, and that the majority of children are not likely to be ready for work involving chord analysis before the age of eleven years.

SUMMARY OF FINDINGS

Before summarizing some of the conclusions we have reached we must again sound a note of caution. Our field of investigation was inevitably limited in terms of both population samples and the abilities measured. This is not to say that we should expect different results from other comparable groups of children; on the contrary, we should expect very similar results. However, since such expectations have not yet been put to further extensive test and *proved* correct, the following conclusions must be read with such limitations in mind; and wherever the expression "musical abilities" is used, it is to be understood as "musical abilities as measured by the tests".

Conclusions

1. Rhythmic memory is more highly developed at all ages of childhood than tonal memory; both appear to be more advanced than keen pitch discrimination; ability to analyse chords develops more slowly than the rest.

2. There is no significant difference between the sexes in musical abilities.

3. Musical abilities in childhood appear to be associated only slightly with intelligence.

4. Musical abilities increase with increase in chronological age throughout childhood, but the average yearly increase is small.

5. At all age levels there is evidence of an extremely wide range of musical abilities.

6. In pitch discrimination the majority of children can accurately discriminate differences of a quarter-tone by the age of seven years; and about half of the ten- and eleven-year-olds, and the majority of twelve-year-olds and older, can discriminate eighth-tones.

7. Pitch discrimination appears to be more accurate on sounds near the middle of the vocal range than on sounds at the extremes of the vocal range or outside it.

8. In tonal memory the last note of each series is the easiest to recall; and chromatic changes—*i.e.*, sounds outside the tonal framework of the established key—are more prominent than whole-tone changes within the tonal framework.

9. The ability to analyse chords is weak in the majority of children below the age of eleven years, but there are some younger children who show ability considerably in excess of the average of their age group.

10 Practical Application of the Findings of the Investigation

Interpretation and speculation—The purpose of music-teaching in school—Sex and musical abilities—Intelligence, chronological age, and musical abilities—Chord analysis—Memory—Pitch discrimination—Postscript

INTERPRETATION AND SPECULATION

In the Preface it was stated that this was a book of ideas and controversial assumptions, of facts, and of speculation. Some of the ideas about musical abilities and their development were discussed in Chapters 1 and 2; the hypotheses underlying the construction of the tests were set out in Chapter 4. The facts, in the form of the results obtained from using the tests, have been set forth in succeeding chapters. It now remains to attempt to interpret these facts in terms of teaching and music-practice, with the school and the classroom in mind; this operation inevitably involves speculation.

THE PURPOSE OF MUSIC-TEACHING IN SCHOOL

Much of what follows in this chapter is connected with ideas on the purpose of music-teaching in schools. I would propose as the purpose of such teaching: the enjoyment of music, leading to its appreciation. Now, appreciation comes as a result of knowledge, and we can only know that with which we have first become acquainted. So the teacher's task is to provide the circumstances in which the pupils will become acquainted with music, then, through repetition, come to know it more intimately, and finally come to 'appreciate' it.

Children become acquainted with and get to know music by listening to it and by taking part in it vocally, instrumentally, or by otherwise moving the body. Bodily movement and singing, as a response to music, are more intimate than instrumental playing; they can take place with no further equipment than nature's own endowment, and are thus under more immediate and subtle control. Now, whether in the form of dance or otherwise, movement *qua* movement is silent. Singing, on the other hand, is a response that involves the two most essential factors in music—pitch and note-lengths. Therefore, whilst acknowledging the important parts that movement and instrumental work can play, for the moment we shall confine our attention to singing; and singing inevitably involves listening.

That which children have sung they are likely to remember better than that to which they have merely listened without positive bodily response. So one good way for children to become acquainted with music is to listen to it, and wherever possible sing what they hear. A common example of this is the teacher singing to a group of five- or six-year-old children, with the children joining in the singing as soon as they have grasped the general shape of the tune. This is rote-learning. The children are hearing, and themselves uttering, the language of music. It requires no formal tuition. Adequate repetition ensures that most will remember what they have heard and sung. We saw this when we were discussing the musical development of children in their early years, in Chapter 2. Also in the same chapter we observed that very young children begin to take an interest in detail, particularly in order to correct, say, a pitch interval which their memory informs them that they are not reproducing accurately. This we called a stage of analysis. By the time a child reaches this stage he has already had considerable acquaintance with the language of music, informally and not necessarily as the result of tuition.

It is when this stage of analysis has been reached in the normal process of maturation, when the child can isolate the two sounds that form a single pitch interval from the rest of the melody, that he can begin to study the language of music in greater detail, and to learn the skills that will eventually enable him to be musically independent of the rote-learning of whole tunes. These skills include learning to name the individual sounds that comprise the pitch intervals with which he is already acquainted through his rote-singing of songs.

All this assumes, of course, that further progress in using the language of music is desirable, and that the pupil is not going to remain at the stage of community singing, entertaining and even uplifting as that might sometimes be. All too often in schools two or even three classes are herded together for what is euphemistically referred to as "a good sing". Usually this is a waste of the pupils' time and of the ratepayers' money. It shows no appreciation of the widely differing musical abilities of individual children, and it is not musical education.

Active participation in music-making leads to greater enjoyment and deeper appreciation, but for any such participation above the most elementary levels some skill in using the language of music is essential. When should we begin teaching these skills, and in what way? Later, in an attempt to answer these questions, I shall refer to data obtained from the investigations I have made. Before doing this, however, let us consider some implications of the findings concerning sex, age, intelligence, and musical abilities.

SEX AND MUSICAL ABILITIES

It appears that there is no difference in the musical abilities of boys and girls in childhood. This confirms the findings of other investigators. Yet it is commonly observed that more girls and young women sing and play instruments than do boys and young men. This may well be due to sociological causes rather than because the female sex is better endowed with musical abilities than the male.

In an environment where music, and especially singing, may be regarded as rather effeminate, young boys may often catch this attitude from older members of their community. Furthermore, boys tend to be more independent than girls, less amenable, and less likely to want to "please the teacher"; in an activity which is possibly considered girlish, boys may become even less co-operative. Doubtless, some of the best child singers are boys; witness cathedral and large church choirs; but such choristers are a tiny minority, and that minority is apparently becoming even smaller, if we are to believe the accounts of the difficulties choirmasters meet in trying to recruit boy singers. Yet, whatever the reason, it is not that there are not enough boys adequately endowed with vocal and musical abilities.

In a school where music lessons occur only once or twice a week, and where these lessons consist entirely of singing songs by rote, it is not to be wondered at if some of the less amenable boys lose interest. If they regard singing itself as girlish they are likely to regard as even more girlish many of the songs they are invited to sing.

Singing is a splendid activity in itself and as a means of becoming acquainted both with the language of music and with a wide repertoire. But mere rote-singing, and nothing else, becomes irksome not only to the less amenable boys, but also to all the more musically able children, girls as well as boys. It is not sufficiently challenging to their developing abilities, and something more is needed. Suggestions as to what this 'something more' might be will follow later in this chapter. The point I wish to stress at the moment is that, as far as we can measure these things, the two sexes, in childhood, are equally endowed with musical abilities.

INTELLIGENCE, CHRONOLOGICAL AGE, AND MUSICAL ABILITIES

The relationship between intelligence and musical abilities was discussed in Chapter 7; there appears to be little connection between them in childhood. Granted comparable musical abilities, opportunity, motivation, tuition, and desire, the more intelligent child is likely to be more successful in music-making than the less intelligent. This could apply to any activity. However, intelligence, as indicated by I.Q., appears to have only slight connection with ability to make the kind

M.A.C.—I

of judgments that we have proposed as fundamental to success in music-making.

We also saw, in Chapter 8, that there is at any given chronological age an enormous range of musical abilities. The wide range of abilities possessed by individual members of a class or group formed mainly on a basis of age and intelligence can present a serious problem for the music teacher.

The grouping, or 'streaming', of children according to their abilities may be to some extent currently unpopular; it is an overt acknowledgment that differences exist between children of the same chronological age. However, denial of the existence of these differences does not eliminate them; and in a system where promotion is by age and not ability, and in which children are taught in large classes—sometimes very large classes in the primary schools—some form of streaming or stratification seems inevitable. Otherwise the brightest and the dullest children in a class suffer boredom on the one hand and discouragement on the other.

The usual criteria for the allocation of children to classes are performance in 'academic' subjects and intelligence, which show a fairly high correlation. Musical abilities and intelligence are not highly correlated, and there appears to be little connection between musical abilities and chronological age; we have revealed very wide differences in musical abilities amongst children of the same chronological age. Thus the normal classification may result in the presence in the same group of children of very high musical abilities and those of extremely low musical abilities.

The grouping of children into classes of fairly limited range of abilities is made on the grounds that it facilitates learning processes in the 'important' subjects, the subjects 'that matter'. Rarely is any attempt made to group children according to their musical abilities. It can be done. The fact that it is not usually done suggests either that administrators are unaware of the wide range of musical abilities that exist at any age, or that music is not regarded as an 'important' subject. Indeed, as we have already seen, not only are children not streamed for music, but, far worse, two or three classes are often put together for 'singing'. This makes it impossible for the teacher to do anything but singing for the whole of the lesson; the sheer bulk of numbers prohibits any other desirable musical activity. Furthermore, under such conditions the teacher cannot possibly get to know the varying abilities of eighty or even a hundred individual pupils.

What, then, can be done? In the first place music must be taught in classes that are at least no larger than the normal class groupings for other subjects such as mathematics or English. This would at least enable the teacher to obtain some knowledge of the abilities of individual children. In the second place, the experiment might be tried of teaching music to children in groups arranged according to musical abilities. Thus, for instance, a child normally in a 'C' stream, on the basis of I.Q. and subjects correlating highly with it, might find himself in an 'A' group for music; and an 'A' stream child might find himself in a 'C' group for music. It could well be that both might be the happier for such an arrangement. There are administrative difficulties, but these are not insuperable.

This suggestion of grouping according to musical abilities is not new; it was championed by Dr Wing some years ago but it has been largely ignored. Since it will probably continue to be ignored, we must in the meantime face the situation as it is, and try to devise ways of doing useful work within the system of class organization that prevails.

Under this system most primary-school classes consist of at least forty pupils, of approximately the same age, but with widely varying abilities. Some will learn much more quickly and effectively than the rest, others correspondingly more slowly and with much greater expenditure of effort. Keeping all happily and purposefully occupied, enabling all to learn and to develop their abilities at their optimum pace, is the class-teacher's constant problem. All class-teaching is a compromise. The compromise is to find work that can be done by the majority whilst neither boring the brighter nor leaving behind the slower. The problem in music is even greater than in many other school subjects.

In order to achieve this compromise, the class-teacher must discover as much as possible about the varying abilities of the individual pupils, and know what may be expected of the majority. Group-tests of musical abilities can provide the teacher with information about both the abilities of individual pupils and the general trends of abilities of the class. They do not tell the whole story, but the information they provide would be otherwise difficult or even impossible to obtain.

We shall now turn to a discussion of the findings concerning the abilities measured by the individual tests, under the headings of chord analysis, memory, and pitch discrimination, and we shall deal with them in that order.

CHORD ANALYSIS

In Chapter 9 we came to the conclusion that, in the majority of children, ability to analyse chords develops more slowly than memory and pitch discrimination; but we also observed that, in a by no means negligible minority of even the youngest children tested, this ability is already far above average for their age group. We might consider these children to be in a category comparable with Revesz's "musically disposed children" who, "even before their first musical instruction, are able to analyse dissonant triads and tetrads with great ease."[1] One of the functions of the test is to discover the more able children. It might well be that the earlier any special abilities are discovered, and given the opportunity for further development, the better for the success and happiness of the child. "The proper time to pick out the gifted individuals is not eleven-plus but as soon as they come up from the infant school."[2] This is especially true in music, where the earlier the necessary skills are discovered and encouraged the better are the chances of success, not necessarily with a view to professional participation, but certainly in terms of personal human satisfaction and development.

However, the tests show that the majority of young children cannot easily analyse concurrent sounds; and this would seem to be in agreement with the statements by Revesz (1953, p. 175) that "children find every harmonic accompaniment equally good, whether consonant or dissonant"; by Valentine (1955, p. 467) that "no appreciable preference for concords before discords is discernible before the (average) age of nine"; by Schoen (1940, p. 230) that "It seems . . . that there is a period of growth when a melody is correctly recognized

[1] Revesz, 1953, p.110, quoted above in Chapter 4, p. 38.
[2] Burt, 1962.

and sung, but harmonic sensitivity is still lacking. For the child up to a certain age, a melody does not carry or imply a certain definite harmonization"; and by Rupp (1915), as quoted by Franklin (1956, p. 55), that "ear for harmony is developed later than the ear for melody."

The purpose of our chord analysis test was not to discover preferences for concord or discord, nor to elicit judgments upon the appropriateness of harmonization, but to measure, in as simple a way as possible, the ability to analyse concurrent sounds.

What is the particular relevance of this information concerning the general lack of ability in chord analysis for the Primary School classroom? It may explain to some extent why, before the age of eleven years, singing in more than one part is rarely encountered, and when it is attempted nearly always proves extremely difficult. Even in the singing of rounds, young children seem to want to shut out the sounds of the other part or parts, sometimes instinctively putting hands over their ears. Progress is even slower and more tedious in attempts to learn songs with two independent parts, especially when the children possess no skill in reading the notation of music.

This must not be understood to imply that young children should not attempt to sing in parts, but at first the material used should be short and easy, and the children must always be given every assistance, aurally and by way of visual symbols as reminders of what they have learnt—*i.e.*, music staff notation, sol-fa, or any other visual device. The more musically able can tackle part-singing earlier than the majority of their contemporaries, and they should be encouraged to do so; on the appropriate occasion they can also help the less able by providing a lead.

Much easier than part-singing is the playing of instruments in parts, especially such tuned pitch-percussion instruments as dulcimers and chime-bars, where the instrument does the tonal thinking. Here the teacher, or the visual symbol, instructs that, for instance, D, F, and A are to be struck; the geographical positions of D, F, and A are known; the actual note-bars may even be marked with their letter names; the bars are struck, and the correct pitches are heard. A chord is the result. In this way children may be helped to apprehend concurrent sounds, and to analyse them. But it must not be forgotten that facility in playing these simple instruments is primarily a facility in manipulation. The instructions are to manipulate, to *do* something, not necessarily to *think*. Tonal thinking, which is the very essence of music, may not even occur. Even where it does occur in elementary instrumental playing it is usually secondary to thinking first about manipulation. In singing, on the other hand, the tonal thinking must come first; this may explain why it is much harder to sing a part moving independently against another part than to play instruments in ensemble.

Memory

The data obtained from our investigations indicate that, by the age of eight years, most children have already reached the stage of analysis in both the tonal and rhythmic aspects of memory; they can remember in sufficient detail to be able to locate the exact place in a tonal configuration or in a rhythmic pattern where a change occurs in the second presentation.

This involves the making of analytical judgments requiring a higher degree of attention to detail than that required in the mere rote-memorization of a frequently repeated melody. It also suggests that, for the majority, from the age of eight years mere rote-memorization of songs may no longer be sufficient challenge to the children's developing abilities. In appropriate ways, then, they should be induced to use these abilities: to pay greater attention to tonal and rhythmic detail, and thus begin to discover for themselves how 'music works' in its basic form of melody.

The evidence of the tests also indicates that chromatic changes are more prominent, and thus more easily perceived, than diatonic changes—*i.e.*, changes within the established tonality. Chromatic changes in the present context are changes of a semitone. This supports the findings of the pitch discrimination test, that the semitone causes little difficulty for most children of seven years of age.

This prominence of the chromatic changes prompts speculation about the development of a feeling for or awareness of tonality. Discussing this development in the child of feeling for tonality, Schoen (1940, p. 226) states:

> . . . up to the sixth year the child grasps tonal relationships only as a general mass impression, so that the reproduction of a melody tone for tone is difficult before that age. During the seventh year signs of a feeling for tonality begin to appear, and it is at this age that children begin to reproduce melodies with correctness of detail, because it is tonality feeling that makes possible the perception, and therefore the correct reproduction, of the simplest formal melodic units.

Franklin (1956, p. 63), in his work on the development of

feeling for tonality, makes special mention of the semitone between the seventh and eighth degrees of the scale:

> . . . we may notice how the transition from the pre-tonal stage to the tonal stage coincides with the child's beginning to use the seventh tone of the scale, and also of his vocal range being widened to the octave and beyond. It seems natural in this connection to remember the trouble the seventh tone caused in the historical period, when the transition began to take place from one-part to multi-part music. In his system of solmization Guido of Arezzo, for instance, was satisfied with hexachords.

Francès (1954), comparing untrained and musically trained adults, concluded that his untrained subjects had no less "expérience auditive des intervalles musicaux" (p. 449) than the musically trained. He speaks of "l'idée . . . d'une acculturation générale existant avant toute éducation technique" (p. 452), from which a feeling for tonality arises.

Although Francès's experiments were with adults, the last-quoted statement is relevant in considering the musical development of young children. Many of the latter seem to have acquired, from environment and incidental experience, an awareness of or feeling for tonality if not "avant toute éducation technique", at least at an early age. This conclusion is supported by Franklin (1956, p. 59) when he states "TMT (*i.e.*, feeling for tonality) is able to stabilize a tonic first at six to nine years." The evidence thus suggests that feeling for tonality is established at an early age, probably by the age of eight years in most children, and possibly much earlier in some. This, of course, may apply only to subjects in the environment of Occidental music culture, in which, as yet, atonal music has not become established as the popular genre.

What the nature of Francès's "acculturation générale" would be in the environment of cultures employing different tonal systems, or possibly in Occidental music of the future, could only be the subject of speculation at the present time.

PITCH DISCRIMINATION

In pitch discrimination we found that the majority of children can accurately discriminate differences of a quarter-tone by the age of seven years; and that about half of the ten- and eleven-year-olds, and the majority of twelve-year-olds and older, can discriminate eighth-tones. This information has relevance for the study of the language of music, commonly but not very accurately referred to as aural training; it is not the physical organ of hearing that is being trained, but the mind. If, under the rather unusual circumstances of this test, where response to the sound stimulus is confined to a judgment and the recording of this in silence, children can accurately discriminate such small pitch differences, including the direction of pitch movement, they are not likely to have difficulty with semitones.

Yet is is sometimes maintained that the semitone, our smallest musical interval, is too difficult for young children to tackle, in spite of the fact that, from a very early age, they often take in their stride both diatonic and chromatic semitones in their own improvisations and in their singing of melodies learnt rotewise. It is true that difficulty may be encountered when the children are asked to concentrate upon the two sounds forming an interval in isolation from the main flow of the tune. But in practice this difficulty is not one of distinguishing between the sounds of the isolated interval, but rather one of naming these sounds. Yet, intrinsically, the naming of the sounds of a semi-tone is no more difficult than the naming of the sounds of a wider interval. No ratiocination is involved. It is merely a question of knowing the names, which, in turn, depends entirely upon rote-memory. However, what has to be memorized must first be learnt; and in this case the learning depends upon the teaching. "What can be named is noticed, is distinguishable from the mass of impression that surrounds."[1] This statement refers to the teaching of language, but it also applies in music-making. If children are not taught how to name the individual sounds of their melodies they have no means of 'distinguishing' these sounds from the mass of 'surrounding impression' in a specific manner such as they themselves can apply in their own individual attempts to come to grips with music. Naming helps that which is perceived to become more specific.

It seems to be generally accepted that, in the process of maturation, children reach 'stages of readiness' for acquiring certain skills, for instance, in reading and number; that the best time for teaching such skills is when these stages of readiness are reached; and that, once the optimum period is passed, subsequent learning and teaching become more arduous and are less likely to meet with success. This theory of stages of readiness also applies in the development of musical skills.

It is the common experience of secondary-school teachers of children of twelve years of age or over that attempts to teach the naming of pitch sounds, which depends entirely upon rote-memorization, meet with only limited success and even at times with resistance. Some older pupils seem to regard

[1] *Primary Education,* 1959.

such rote-memorization as childish and beneath them. It would appear that they have already passed the optimum period for such an operation.

Even amongst ten- and eleven-year-old pupils in primary schools some boys and girls appear to resent work which they feel, perhaps quite subconsciously, to be more appropriate for younger children. Furthermore, some teachers report a decrease of interest in music-making amongst children of this age, particularly amongst those who have not already acquired elementary skills that they can apply themselves in the further development of their music-making. As we have already indicated, the mere rote-learning of unison songs is no longer sufficiently challenging to their developing abilities, and the learning of part songs by rote is even more tedious.

We have proposed that the naming of pitch sounds is essential for progress in the use of the language of music, and it would appear that the optimum period for acquiring the skills of naming is in the earlier years of the primary school. We may now consider possible ways of teaching such skills.

How we teach the naming of the sounds, and what names we use, depends to some extent upon the point of view, or even upon the skill and knowledge, of the teacher. The absolute pitch names, A, B, C, . . . G, are of little use for the majority of young children. Absolute pitch is a form of memory possessed by few, and as yet no reliable method of teaching it to others has been found. For most children, and adults, the naming of intervals is a function of relative, and not absolute, pitch.

For the purpose of naming in relative pitch, numbers are

possible, but they take no account of chromatic semitones. Solfège, with its fixed 'doh' or 'ut', suffers from the same limitation. Sol-fa syllables, which are not tied to a fixed pitch, are monosyllabic throughout both the diatonic and chromatic steps, and are at the same time simple and logical. Very young children learn them easily, when taught by one who knows them thoroughly and uses them musically. Once thoroughly mastered, these 'singing names' may be applied to any key; they become, as it were, a personal, portable keyboard that never goes out of tune.

Our investigations provide an indication of the order in which the naming of pitch intervals might best be made. The pilot test of pitch discrimination showed semitones to be more difficult to judge than whole-tones, and whole-tones more difficult than larger intervals. This suggests that analytical work involving the naming of the sounds should begin with larger intervals. Of such larger intervals, the minor third has been found to be the one most commonly used by very young children in their 'chants' (see Chapter 2). It also proved to be the easiest of the items in the thirty-chord test described earlier (Chapter 6, p. 64).[1] It would seem reasonable, therefore, to take this interval as the starting-point in learning to name the sounds of the language of music.

Once the minor third and the names of its sounds have been firmly established, other intervals may be added, one by one,

[1] It is interesting to note that, whereas the minor third was the easiest item in the thirty-chord test, the major third had proved to be almost three times as difficult, and, apart from a four-note chord, the most difficult item of the test. For this reason it was eliminated in the latest version of the chord analysis test. (See Chapter 6, p. 64.)

until the whole of the pentatonic scale is in use. The stages are as follows:

Stage I	II	III	IV	V
				(d¹)
	l	l	l	l
s	s	s	s	s
m	m	m	m	m
		r	r	r
			d	d
				l₁

Some songs suitable for young children use only the sounds of the pentatonic scale; and at all the stages children and teacher can additionally devise their own songs, making use of the sounds they have learnt to name in live music-making. Such songs should be used extensively at each stage.[1] Obviously there is no useful purpose in teaching a scale, or any other theoretical knowledge or skills, that is not applied in real music; and "real music" for children includes that which they make up themselves.

It will be observed that the pentatonic scale contains no semitones. When the whole-tones and larger intervals of the pentatonic scale, together with names for the sounds, are well

[1] This does not imply that songs based on the sounds of the pentatonic scale are the only ones to be sung. We have already seen that children naturally use a wider vocabulary of sounds, including chromatics, in their improvisations and songs learnt rotewise. But at this particular stage of learning to name the pitch sounds of the language of music, songs based on the pentatonic scale are especially useful.

established, semitones (t₁ d and m f) may then be added. The
following octave scale is now available:

$$
\begin{array}{c}
l \\
s \\
f \\
m \\
r \\
d \\
t_1 \\
l_1
\end{array}
$$

together with octave repeats (*e.g.*, upper t and d¹) as required.

It may be noted that this scale is not the diatonic major
scale which is usually taught first in schools, and sometimes is
the only scale taught. It is the descending form of the melodic
minor, otherwise the Aeolian mode. This form is proposed as
the first octave scale to be built up, because it is just as easy to
teach as the diatonic major scale, and because it can become
either the melodic minor in its ascending form or the diatonic
major with a minimum of transference or alteration. No alteration is needed for the descending form of the minor. Only two
alterations are needed for the ascending form of the minor, ba
and se. (These are pronounced 'bay' and 'see'. Ba is the single
characteristic sound of the ascending minor scale, leading upward, not a semitone as fe,—*i.e.*, the sharpened fah—would
indicate, but a whole-tone to the sharpened seventh, se.) For
use as the diatonic major scale, mere transference of the low t₁
an octave up, and the upper octave repeat of d, is all that is
necessary. Children experience no difficulty with octave trans-
ferences of sounds whose names they already know; and the
sounds of and names for ba and se are just as easy to teach

as any other degrees of the scale. Again, it is merely a matter of rote-memorization. Here, then, are the three scales side by side:

		d¹
		t
l	l	l
	se	
s		s
	ba	
f		f
m	m	m
r	r	r
d	d	d
t₁	t₁	
l₁	l₁	

Once these are firmly established in use, chromatics may be added as needed. Whenever a new sound is added, together with its name, it should be used extensively in actual music. We would stress again that there is no virtue in a scale *qua* scale, but only in the use that can be made of it, or of its constituent parts, in live music-making.

We have already pointed out that the naming of different pitch sounds depends upon rote-memory; the 'singing names' have to be taught. Furthermore, they are useless until the association of sound and name for it have become automatic. To achieve this automatic association frequent and regular practice is needed.

In his own language development the child not only hears the language spoken daily, but, in order to satisfy his needs, he himself also speaks it daily, at certain stages apparently all day! He gets constant practice. In his musical development it is true that he may *hear* much music in the home and school, but he is not necessarily *listening*; and only comparatively rarely does he himself utter—*i.e.*, sing—the music that he hears. Even more rarely, and in some cases apparently never, does he attend analytically to the constituent sounds of music, pitch intervals, and note-lengths. Yet this he must do if he is to make any independent progress in the language of music. Thus it falls to the teacher to provide the opportunity and the stimulus, and to ensure that he is given regular practice.

We have dealt at some length with the pitch factor. Other factors are important, but the pitch factor is the most important. Without it music does not exist. In music education it must have pride of place. Yet it is often neglected; teaching of the skills needed for dealing with the pitch factor is often omitted, or started too late, when the stage of readiness has already passed. We have suggested a method of approach that has been proved effective; it is not the only method. But whatever method is used, it must be at the right time. The stage of readiness must not be missed. The evidence we have obtained from our investigations indicates that as early as seven years of age the majority of children are ready to tackle the kind of work we have suggested in the foregoing pages.

POSTSCRIPT

The facts have been stated; the hypotheses upon which the experiments were based have been set out; we have attempted to interpret the findings in terms of classroom practice. The interpretation is open to challenge. It has been made in the hope that it will be challenged; for the person who challenges is thinking; he is stirred; and from the turmoil something better may emerge.

M.A.C.—K

We have not been concerned with the whole of musical development and education, nor with musical ability as a whole, but only with such aspects of it that we were able to measure in young children. However, these aspects, like the other issues raised in this book, are fundamental. They demand more than superficial thought. If the book has caused the reader to think more deeply, and sends him to some of the references listed in the bibliography, it will have served at least one useful purpose.

Bibliography of Works cited in the Text

ANASTASI, A. (1954): *Psychological Testing* (New York: Macmillan).

BENTLEY, A. (1963): "A study of some aspects of musical ability amongst young children, including those unable to sing in tune" (Unpublished thesis. University of Reading Library).

BURT, C. (1962): "The Gifted Child—Psychological Evidence" (*Times Ed. Suppl.*, 26 Jan. 1962, p. 125).

DYSON, G. (1954): *Fiddling while Rome burns* (London: O.U.P.).

FARNSWORTH, P. R. (1958): *The Social Psychology of Music* (New York: Dryden Press).

FRANCÈS, R. (1954): "Recherches expérimentales sur la perception de la mélodie" (*J. Psychol. norm. path.*, 47–51, 439–457).

FRANKLIN, E. (1956): *Tonality as a Basis for the Study of Musical Talent* (Göteborg, Sweden: Gumpert).

HENKIN, R. I. (1957): "Re-evaluation of a factorial study of the components of music" (*J. Psychol.*, 43, 301–306).

KWALWASSER, J. (1927): *Tests and Measurements in Music* (Boston: Birchard).

KWALWASSER, J. (1955): *Exploring the Musical Mind* (New York: Coleman-Ross).

LOWERY, H. (1952): *The Background of Music* (London: Hutchinson).

LUNDIN, R. W. (1953): *An Objective Psychology of Music* (New York: Ronald Press).

MOORHEAD, G. and POND, D. (1941): "Music of Young Children—Chant" (Pillsbury Foundation Studies No. 1, 1611 Anacapa St, Santa Barbara, California).

MURSELL, J. L. and GLENN, M. (1931): *The Psychology of School Music Teaching* (New York: Silver Burdett).

ORTMANN, O. (1926): "On the melodic relativity of tones" (*Psychol. Monogr.* 35, No. 1, 1–47).

PRIMARY EDUCATION (1959): "Suggestions for the consideration of teachers and others concerned with the work of Primary Schools" (London: H.M.S.O.).

REVESZ, G. (1925): *The Psychology of a Musical Prodigy* (London: Kegan Paul).

REVESZ, G. (1953): *Introduction to the Psychology of Music* (London: Longmans).

RUPP, H. (1915): "Über die Prüfung musikalischer Fähigkeiten" —Teil I Z aug Ps., 1915, 9, 1–76.

SCHOEN, M. (1940): *The Psychology of Music* (New York: Ronald Press).

SEASHORE, C. E. (1938): *Psychology of Music* (New York: McGraw Hill).

SEASHORE, C. E. (1939): *Measures of Musical Talent* (1939 revision) and Manual of Instructions (Camden, N. J.: R.C.A. Victor Division).

SHUTER, R. P. G. (1964): "An investigation of hereditary and environmental factors in musical ability" (Ph.D. thesis. University of London Library).

SPEARMAN, C. (1927): *The Abilities of Man* (London: Macmillan).

SUMNER, W. L. (1948): *Statistics in School* (Oxford: Blackwell).

VALENTINE, C. W. (1955): *Psychology and its Bearing on Education* (London: Methuen).

VERNON, P. E. (1932): "The Apprehension and Cognition of Music" (*Proc. of Mus. Assoc.* LIX, 1932–33, pp. 61–84).

WING, H. D. (1947): "Standardised Tests of Musical Intelligence" (Sheffield: City Training College).

WING, H. D. (1948): "Tests of Musical Ability and Appreciation" (*B.J.Psychol. Monogr. Supp.* No. 27: C.U.P.).

WING, H. D. (1956): "The Measurement of Musical Aptitude" (*Occup. Psychol.* 31, 1 Jan. 1957, pp. 33–37).

Index

The principal references are shown in **bold** type